2004 POE

ONCE UPON A RHYME

IMAGINATION FOR A NEW GENERATION

Central England Vol II
Edited by Claire Tupholme

 Young**Writers**

First published in Great Britain in 2004 by:
Young Writers
Remus House
Coltsfoot Drive
Peterborough
PE2 9JX
Telephone: 01733 890066
Website: www.youngwriters.co.uk

SB ISBN 1 84460 619 8

Foreword

Young Writers was established in 1991 and has been passionately devoted to the promotion of reading and writing in children and young adults ever since. The quest continues today. Young Writers remains as committed to engendering the fostering of burgeoning poetic and literary talent as ever.

This year's Young Writers competition has proven as vibrant and dynamic as ever and we are delighted to present a showcase of the best poetry from across the UK. Each poem has been carefully selected from a wealth of *Once Upon A Rhyme* entries before ultimately being published in this, our twelfth primary school poetry series.

Once again, we have been supremely impressed by the overall high quality of the entries we have received. The imagination, energy and creativity which has gone into each young writer's entry made choosing the best poems a challenging and often difficult but ultimately hugely rewarding task - the general high standard of the work submitted amply vindicating this opportunity to bring their poetry to a larger appreciative audience.

We sincerely hope you are pleased with our final selection and that you will enjoy *Once Upon A Rhyme Central England Vol II* for many years to come.

Contents

Beth Cunningham (8)	19
Jessica Hamilton (8)	19
Jordan Simcock (8)	20
Barry Jones (9)	20
Craig Jones (9)	21
Danica Craddock (8)	21
Luke Hoddle (9)	22
Naomi Baskerville (9)	22

Chaucer Junior School, Ilkeston

Rachel Meer (11)	23
Emily Corns (8)	23
Jason Blackman (9)	24
Polly Love (8)	24
Jessé-Mae Breame (9)	25
Isabella Hawkes (8)	26
Aaron Brown (9)	26
Loui Watson (8)	27
James Harrison (8)	27
Jade Scarborough (10)	28
Peta Brown (8)	28
Byron Fitchett (8)	29
Kay Mather (9)	29
Louise Draper (9)	30
Thomas Robinson (10)	31
Ben Massey (9)	31
Samuel Jones (9)	32
Natasha Williams (10)	32
Alexandra Beviss (9)	33
Nada Baker (10)	33
Chloe Crawshaw (10)	34
Kyran Deakin (10)	34
Jacob Robinson (10)	35
Brendon Limb (9)	36
Carmel Eyre (11)	37
Shelby Boyles (10)	37
Jake Dean (10)	38
Cameron Scarle (10)	38
Louis Clegg (10)	39
Ellie Bednall (10)	39
Jack Andrews (11)	40

Jamie Chaplin (10)	40
Daniel Briggs (9)	41
Joshua Price (10)	42
Christina Jackson (11)	43
Laurie Trueman (10)	44
Sean Green (10)	44
Jack Hallam (11)	45
Jamie Gingell (10)	45
Jessica Frost (10)	46
Elliot Johnson (10)	46
Louise Smith (10)	47
Paige Bradshaw (9)	47
Sam Tuck (9)	48
Connor Page (10)	48
Rebecca Heywood (8)	49
Ellie Thompson (10)	49
Ben Connelly (10)	50
Scott Eyre (9)	50
Kirsty Nadin (9)	51
Marcus Woollands (10)	51
Alice Macqueen (9)	52
Kelly Barker (8)	52
Courtney Reeve (8)	53
Stefan May (9)	53
Lauren Roberts (9)	54
Brendan Gough (7)	54
Jake Ledger (9)	55
Kayleigh Waller (10)	55
Daniel Gale (9)	56
Jordan Green (10)	56
Dale Nind (8)	57
Cannon Oakley-Thorpe (9)	57
Hannah Heywood (10)	58
Joe Taylor (8)	58
Katie Meer (8)	59
Ben French (9)	59

Coten End Primary School, Warwick

Stacey Ellis (11)	60
Emma O'Dwyer (10)	61
James Gillett (11)	62

Guy Joseph (11)	63
Lucy Edwards (10)	63
Georgina Lamb (11)	64
Martin Brown (11)	64
Abigail Smith-Howells (11)	65
Kimberley Williams (10)	65
Tim Hood (11)	66
Danielle Scott (11)	67
Amy-Louise Morgan (11)	67
Ben Miller & Joshua Baker (11)	68
Charlotte Lilley (11)	68
Edward McEwan (10)	69
Rebecca Robinson (10)	69
Prashant Roka (11)	70
James Shacklock (11)	70
Hannah Ingram (11)	71
Lewis Coulson (10)	71
Jonathan James (11)	72
Sira Mahmood (11)	72
Faye Herrington (11)	73
Charlotte Marshall (11)	73
Cameron Ferguson (11)	74
Catherine Pitchford (10)	74
Ashleigh O'Connor (11)	74
Hannah Gregg (10)	75
Hannah Green (11)	75
Amrita Jhaj (11)	76
Katy Lawrence (11)	76
Beth Williams (10)	76
Kirsty Baker (11)	77
Lindsey Bolitho (11)	77
Lewis Mowat (11)	77
James Ward (11)	78
Ricardo Spratt (11)	78
Laura Cunningham (11)	79
Matthew Bennett (11)	79

Croft Junior School, Nuneaton

Chloe Morris (7)	80
Kelly Lobley (7)	80
Kelsey Collins (7)	81

Lucy Clarke (10)	82
Sarah Timms (8)	83
Amy Bell (8)	84
Connor Whitmore-Lewis (7)	85
Owen Woodward (8)	86
Cody Clarke (7)	87
Chloe Tedds (7)	88
Laura Harrison (8)	89
Nathan Aston (8)	90
Megan Farmer (8)	91
Jake Cleghorn (8)	92
Keri-Ann Bishop (8)	93
Faye Glover (8)	94
Lucy Fitzsimmons (7)	95

Ewyas Harold Primary School, Hereford

Ty Marshall	95
Jasmine King (11)	96
Christopher Talbot (10)	96

Hall Green Junior School, Birmingham

Sammi-Jo Lowe (9)	97
James Fry (9)	97
Emily Kennedy (9)	98
Katie Clarke-Mullen (9)	98
Damini Dave (9)	99
Alison Colgan (8)	99
Sannah Mehmood (8)	100
Kurt Morris (9)	100
Zoe Tibbetts (8)	101
Faisal Qureshi (9)	101
Arjun Modhwadia (8)	102

Haselor School, Alcester

Daniel De Rosa (10)	102
Emily Harrison (10)	103
Sebastian Young (11)	104
Nicola Boots (11)	104
Jordan Clarke (10)	104
Helen Geddy (11)	105

Louis Randall (11)	105
Lewis Seabright (11)	105
Emily Bennett (10)	106
Ben Jackson (10)	106
Nicholas Gardener (10)	106
Jessica Rice (11)	107
Phoebe Parkes (9)	107
Joshua Kitchen (11)	108
Luke Nicholson (10)	108
Gabby Cook (11)	109

Hillmorton Primary School, Rugby

Scott Corbett (10)	109
Adam Stevens (10)	110
Jason Fulthorpe (8)	110
Jack Stewardson (10)	111
Scott Webb (11)	112
Lauren Kennedy (10)	112
Naomi Scarsbrook (10)	113
Amy Kennedy (10)	113
Susan Billingham (10)	114
Charlotte Butcher (10)	114
Thomas Millett (9)	115
Tommie Harris (11)	115
Samantha Clarke (10)	115
Tommy Hall (11)	116
Katherine Cooney (10)	116
Russell Pinks (11)	117
Liam Moore (9)	117
Reece Tranter (10)	118
Olivia Abbott (11)	118
Jamie Newman (10)	118
William Ratcliffe (10)	119
Willow Harris (9)	119
Alex Walker (11)	120
Emily Mann (8)	120
Sarah Parsons (11)	121
Madalaine Vale (9)	121
Sophie Jones (11)	122
Sarah Collier (11)	122
Emma Staley (10)	122

Newcroft Primary School, Shepshed

Old Vicarage School, Derby

St Joseph's Catholic School, Malvern

St Oswald's CE Primary School, Rugby

Ashton Branston (10)	179
Sujahn Barhey (8)	179
Bethany McLaren (10)	180
Jordana Lawes (10)	180
Marianne Willey (10)	181
Rory Absalom (8)	181
Alexander Jordan (7)	182
Alice Allett (7)	183
Zachary Rees (9)	184
Kieran Taylour (10)	184
Rory Hanby (9)	185
Lauren Scott (7)	185
Kyle Cooper (8)	186
Kya Harris (8)	187
Lauren Ross (8)	187
Toni Rotheram (8)	188
Thomas Branston (8)	188
Kyle Bowden (10)	189
Luis Holloway (9)	189
Shivani Koria (7)	190
Ciaran Wardle (8)	190
Ben Romasz (8)	191
Sarita Sihra (8)	191

The Croft School, Stratford-Upon-Avon

Henry Lougher (9)	191
Ellie Sergeant (11)	192
Louise Keegan (10)	192
Naomi Nixon (11)	192
Elizabeth Cawthorn (10)	193
Lucy Martin (11)	193
Ian Howard (11)	194
James Page (10)	194
Portia Conn	194
Andrew Turton (10)	195
Felicity Box (11)	195
Jenny Morris (11)	196
Jamie Thomas (10)	196
Mark Tagliaferri (11)	197
Ellie Forman (10)	197

Peter Walters (11)   198
Alex Hughes (10)   198
Catherine Lawler (11)   199
Emma Walshe (10)   199
Mark Dove (11)   200

Welford On Avon Primary School, Stratford-Upon-Avon
Emily Aveyard   200
Daniel Walsh (9)   201
Eleanor Johnston (10)   201
Jessica Summer (9)   202
Harry White (9)   202
Lucas Spence   203
Jennifer Lane (9)   203
Morgan Jackson (9)   204
James Clifford (9)   204

The Poems

Dove Cottage

Dove Cottage standing tall and proud,
Walk onto the stone-cold floor,
Hear the wind blowing loud,
It sounds like an animal's roar!

The orange-red fire making a crackling sound,
Wordsworth and Johnny snug in their beds,
Curtains shut, no movement can be found,
Johnny's dreaming wonderful adventures in his head.

Lots of windows all so small,
Listen to the door creaking,
Step into the posh, quaint hall,
Are there any mice squeaking?

In the garden, flowers come from the soil,
The wind is blowing them side to side,
Twisting ivy growing round in a coil,
Watch as the sparrows glide.

Leah Huddleston, Georgia Powell & Jessica Birbeck (9)
Birds Bush CP School, Tamworth

Furness Abbey

The abbey is so quiet
And extremely still,
I am sitting on a rock
And the wind is giving me a chill.

The creepy staircase,
With bumps and cracks.
The bricks swirl around
In bumpy tracks.

The grass is boggy
And also soggy.
Its built on oak tree trunks
And was made by the monks.

Charlotte Kerridge & Laura-Jay Harris (8)
Birds Bush CP School, Tamworth

Gathering Shells

On Warmly Beach,
Amongst our feet.
We gather shells,
Inhaling their smells.

Seagulls' wings flapping,
Elderly people napping.
Crunching of the sand,
Tickles my tiny hand.

The waves are lapping,
The children are chattering.
Freshly-made sandwiches,
Wrapped in neat packages.

Slimy seaweed tickles my feet,
As my brother tucks in to eat.
Dad drinking a cool refreshing beer,
The water deepens I have no fear.

The sun begins to set,
Time to dry off the wet.
Climb into the dry
And wave goodbye.

Jemma Broadstock & Carly Thompson (8)
Birds Bush CP School, Tamworth

The Abbey

I am the abbey, still standing tall,
The monks made me strong, so I wouldn't fall.
In the lush green grass I can still be found,
People come to visit from miles around.

Monks' ghosts still wander my path,
I often hear a quiet laugh,
My land covered in oak,
The sun beaming like a large round yolk.

My bricks thick and strong,
The stream trickles along,
The monks' ghosts still wander around,
But quietly and don't make a sound.

Ellie Stevens (8)
Birds Bush CP School, Tamworth

The Docks

The boat in the harbour is very still,
Its driver carefully steps on deck.
The air is eerie, there is a chill,
Ropes and engines all in check.

The engine begins to rumble,
The old boat comes to life.
The fading dock's sounds,
Amongst the waves - the sea's wildlife.

Turning round in the distance,
The fishermen could see the docks.
The towering cranes still in existence,
Overhead the seagulls flock.

Harry Bird (7), Jack Brown & Lee Carter (9)
Birds Bush CP School, Tamworth

Warmly Channel Beach

Playing on the beach,
I caught a leech,
Climbing on the rocks,
I've got dirty socks.

It cost a whole penny
To see my friend Jenny,
We gathered shells, massive and round,
Oh! What beautiful things we've found.

Getting into my bathing clothes,
I get sand amongst my toes,
I saw something swimming in the sea,
What wonderful things could it be?

The sun sets,
I shake off the wet,
I've got my beautiful shells,
I rattle them like bells.

Devon Lee & Antony Bretherton (8)
Birds Bush CP School, Tamworth

Furness Abbey

The creatures creep and crawl
As they climb my broken wall
They make their homes
On my bumpy stones.

Here I am standing still
The monks built me on a hill
They left me here as they passed away
Now this is where I have to stay.

When Henry came
He blew me down like a game
He wanted to make me his,
He stole all the monks' riches.

Bethanie D'Arcy & Keelyann Carter (9)
Birds Bush CP School, Tamworth

The Abbey

The water flowing gently,
The birds singing intelligently,
The bumpy pathway,
The abbey is still here today.

The uneven wall,
The doors are now so small,
The mud on the ground,
The sounds all around.

The very spooky alleys,
The little nooks and crannies,
The fresh water river,
The abbey makes me quiver.

The lush green grass,
The broken pieces of glass,
The huge tree trunks,
The ghosts of the monks.

Stacie McDonald (8)
Birds Bush CP School, Tamworth

Furness Abbey

The abbey is so quiet
And extremely still,
I am sitting on a rock
The wind gives me a chill.

The lush green grass,
The big brocken rocks,
The huge tree trunks,
The ghost of the monks.

The brocken walls,
The fresh spring water,
The oak flooring,
The sound of nature.

Bethany Noble (8)
Birds Bush CP School, Tamworth

The Ancient Abbey

The abbey has aged, over the mysterious years,
The delicate walls stand tall and proud,
We hide our ancient treasure in dark tunnels.

Staircases tall and wide made out of cold stone,
Metal bars that are as cold as ice,
The grass looks fresh with newly-sprouted daisies.

Midnight dreams of better days,
When we awake our hearts shall fade,
In Heaven above we send our love
To the children that play,
When we die our spirits will fly
And watch over the abbey forever.

Sarah Boxall (7) & Aliyah Reid (9)
Birds Bush CP School, Tamworth

On Warmly Channel Beach

On Warmly Beach we gather shells,
Inhaling all their different smells,
The ripples of the water
Refreshes my toes, the sun's a scorcher.

The crunching of the sand,
Scattered all over the land.
People are busily talking
And seagulls are loudly squawking.

Step-stone across the sea,
'Cause Mum's lost her penny.
The water is whooshing in,
I have found an old, ugly tin.

Gracie Lawson & Grace Clarke (8)
Birds Bush CP School, Tamworth

The Great Abbey

The abbey so quiet,
With all nature's sounds.
The birds are fluttering
Quietly around.

The lush green grass,
Bathing in the sun.
The stream so splashy
And a lot of fun.

The abbey so still,
Can't hear a mouse,
But only when they
Come out of their house.

The creepy staircase
With all its bumps
Its mysterious spirals
With lumps like camels' humps.

The arched doors
Still standing tall,
Pictures of monks
Hanging on the wall.

Louise Carroll & Chloe Ravenscroft (9)
Birds Bush CP School, Tamworth

Colours

Blue is like a rushing river
Pink is as light as a pen
Purple is like ink flowing on the table
Yellow is like our spelling books
Black is like the darkness of the night
Orange is like a bright orange
Brown is like a lonely shelf.

Calum Brotherston (8)
Boughton Leigh Junior School, Rugby

Home From School

Seeing the door before I'm through it,
Seeing the TV ready to be turned on,
Seeing the stairs that I go up to the PlayStation,
Seeing the kitchen with all the sweets in,
Seeing the open windows letting cool air in,
Seeing tea on the table, a plateful to eat.

Tasting the biscuits before my tea,
Tasting the squash when I need a drink,
Tasting some sweets but I'm still hungry,
Tasting water just before my tea,
Tasting pizza, chips and beans for my tea,
Tasting some chocolate cake for my pudding.

Hearing the birds sing their song,
Hearing my brother walk through the door,
Hearing the turned on oven cooking for me,
Hearing school bags hit the floor,
Hearing people talking on the TV.

Andrew Clowes (9)
Boughton Leigh Junior School, Rugby

Spring

Smell of spring in the sweet warm air,
Newborn lambs leaping everywhere,
Pretty daffodils peeping out into the spring sky,
Hats and scarves thrown on the ground,
Children playing with a happy sound,
Laughing, dancing for all to see,
Some skipping round a tree,
Having a picnic all with glee,

Spring's my favourite time of year!

Hannah Birch (9)
Boughton Leigh Junior School, Rugby

Spring

Birds are singing
And I am pinging

Lawnmowers are mowing
And I am showing

Baby lambs being born
And there is the dawn

People are going out
I don't half shout

Flowers are popping
I am hopping

It's getting very, very hot
I'm making a pot

There are longer days
And stacks of hay.

Jake Everitt (9)
Boughton Leigh Junior School, Rugby

Home From School Senses

I see my mum standing at the door,
Ethan crawling on the floor.
I hear two brothers being pests,
Only just finished a bunch of tests,
I smell dinner cooking slowly,
The two brothers now not lonely,
I taste tuna pasta bake
With a cup of chocolate milkshake,
I open the door
And put my stuff on the floor.

Jordan Cawley (8)
Boughton Leigh Junior School, Rugby

Safari Park

Penguins huddle in a bunch,
All to get their fishy lunch.

Monkeys swing on vines
And sound like clock chimes.

Kangaroos jump up high,
Sometimes I think they're going to fly.

The tortoise is slow,
But he can eat a bow.

The lion's in a pride,
But sometimes he steps aside.

You can go to see the bunny,
But I warn you, he's very funny.

Come and see the seal
And watch him have his meal.

The fox is very sly
And jumps up high.

A mole likes digging
And likes escaping.

Zebra herds move around,
Going swiftly along the ground.

Snakes slither across the floors
And try to slither under doors.

Lions in a cage,
But still come from a mighty age.

The mother elephant has a daughter
And sprays her with lots of water.

The giraffe's really tall,
You'll have to throw it high to make them catch a ball.

And the crocodiles decide to mate
And all crawl out the gate.

Goodbye with the crocodiles and the ark,
So make sure you come back to the safari park.

Eleanor Prior (9)
Boughton Leigh Junior School, Rugby

Spring

Spring is bright
Is so light
Newborn lambs
Relaxing in their fields
Leaves growing on trees
In the gentle breeze
The storms have gone
And the air is here
Waking the animals
From their long winter sleep.

Ryan Cosgrove (9)
Boughton Leigh Junior School, Rugby

Spring

Spring is a brand new season
The flowers are peeping
Through the fresh green grass
Children are playing
Mums and dads are gardening
New flowers are growing
Birds singing, cats playing with butterflies
Animals wake from a long winter sleep
Baby lambs are born and learn how to walk.

Hannah Davies (9)
Boughton Leigh Junior School, Rugby

Senses Poem

Hearing my next-door neighbour shouting my name
Hearing the clear words on the television
Hearing the kettle boil for my mum's tea
Hearing the cooker alarm go off when dinner is ready

Seeing a brown back door before me
Seeing the dirty and clean windows
Seeing the still, wooden tables ready for tea
Seeing the black TV ready to watch

Touching the silver cold handle on the door
Touching the hard buttony remotes to turn on the TV
Touching my favourite game Swingball

Tasting my tea, *mmm, mmm*
Tasting my drink - pink grapefruit
Tasting my pudding - a yoghurt or two
Tasting chewy sweets.

Leila Jennings (9)
Boughton Leigh Junior School, Rugby

Daffodils

D affodils, daffodils swaying in the breeze
A ll of them dancing round willow trees
F lowing daffodils, flowing for you and me
F inding the spring again, come along and see
O pening their buds, awakening from their sleep
D ressing themselves in yellow petals
I n crumbling soil now they peep
L ong green stems and buds that peer
S pring's my favourite time of year!

Niamh Gold (8)
Boughton Leigh Junior School, Rugby

Home From School

Smelling -
Smelling fresh coffee from the coffee pot
That my mum and dad are drinking,
Smelling my mum's perfume
When I give her a hug,
Smelling pot pourri in the living room,
Smelling my mum's flowers on the kitchen table.

Hearing -
Hearing the TV
Hearing my mum say, 'Had a good day at school?'
Hearing my little sister say hello,
Hearing my dad saying, 'Want anything to eat or drink?'

Seeing -
Seeing the stairs and the bright purple carpet
Seeing my mum and little sister
Seeing the kitchen
Seeing the table and chairs
Seeing the dazzling pink toaster
Seeing my two goldfish, Salt and Pepper
Swimming merrily in their tank

Tasting -
Tasting my prawn cocktail flavour crisps
Tasting my drink of Coke
Tasting my chocolate cake
Tasting my doughnut
Tasting my pizza and chips
Tasting my chocolate ice cream.

Michaela Morris (9)
Boughton Leigh Junior School, Rugby

Blue

Blue is the sea
Shining back at me,
Blue is socks
With polka dots,
Blue is veins
The colour of rain,
Blue is cold ice
And the colour of your eyes,
Blue is socks
But not chickenpox,
Blue is cold
That you can't hold,
Blue is a stained glass window
And the colours of my pillow,
Blue is a crisp packet
And a football kit,
Blue is shoes
But not chocolate mousse,
The world could not be true
Without blue.

Liam Soper (9)
Boughton Leigh Junior School, Rugby

Daffodils

D ancing daffodils singing happily
A nd swaying side to side
F lowing swiftly singing away
F ight with a strong wind
O r blow in the warm breeze
D emons fly above their heads
I love daffodils red, hot and yellow
L ive for and pray for them
S ome have to die but there will be some next year.

Dale Harris (9)
Boughton Leigh Junior School, Rugby

The Ark Safari Park

Penguins huddle in a bunch
To catch their icy lunch.

Monkeys swing from vines
And sound like clock chimes.

Kangaroos jump so high,
I think they're going to fly!

The tortoise is really slow,
He can eat a bow.

The lion's in a pride,
Sometimes he steps aside.

You can see a bunny,
But he's not very funny.

Come and see the giant seal
And watch him eat a fishy meal.

The fox is cunning
But he doesn't like running.

A mole likes digging holes.

Goodbye from the ark,
But come back to the safari park.

Emilie Weaver (9)
Boughton Leigh Junior School, Rugby

Warning! Dangerous Dirty Dan

Dirty Dan steals cars
He puts on a jet-pack and flies to Mars
He meets some aliens and pretends to be a friend
He explored the planet and found some hens
He flew to the sun and fried, oh no, he died!

Sam Draper (9)
Boughton Leigh Junior School, Rugby

Shadows

Shadows are of mystery
Shadows are a lie
Shadows can be terrifying
Shadows can make you cry.

Shadows are quite frustrating
Shadows are of the doomed
Shadows are unknown
Shadows are of where light once loomed.

The shadows are fading
The shadows have disappeared
The light is now returning
The light has now appeared.

Thomas Peverelle (9)
Boughton Leigh Junior School, Rugby

Billy Came To An End

He was very amusing but did not get far
He crashed the car
And fell in tar
He went to the bar
To get a car
He eats a wheel
But it was steel
The steering wheel was being crunched
He died and never had lunch again.

Demi Ashwell (8)
Boughton Leigh Junior School, Rugby

Daffodils

D affodils blowing in the breeze,
A ll in unison with the trees,
F leeting glimpses of summer to come,
F or you and me and everyone,
O ut of the ground they poke their heads,
D ressing lawns and flower beds,
I n time they lose their yellow blooms,
L ike all before have returned to earthy tombs,
S urely to come again next year to bring us all the best of cheer!

Chloe Westerby (8)
Boughton Leigh Junior School, Rugby

Night

Squeaky noises heard late at night,
Frogs and toads yelling for play,
Gales screeching!
Conkers smashing on the ground,
Branches flying across the street,
Terrifying eyes and noises all around,
Hands of the dead hitting me on the head,
Freezing, wet, petrifying feeling,
Burning and smoky men falling to the ground,
Seeing ladies tripping over,
Raining, flamy air killing,
Sweating all over,
Smelling flames, drink and food,
Something creeping around the street,
Ah! Finally home,
Oh! Christmas tree lights!
I'm happy!

Jason Haywood (8)
Carmountside Primary School, Stoke-on-Trent

Night

People creeping in the dark,
Wolves and foxes spying on me,
Shadows around me!

Spooky trees with sword claws,
Eyes watching me everywhere I go,
Tree fingers touching my shoulder,
Piano noises of the dead,
Freezing like ice cubes,
Fear on me,
Smelling fumes, food and dirt,
Finally my friend's house,
Goosebumps have gone from me.

Connor Hancock (8)
Carmountside Primary School, Stoke-on-Trent

Night

Creepy eyes following me,
Footsteps right beside me,
Imagining hands touching you,
Tree arms and mouths and eyes moving,
Something talking to me,
Seeing razor-sharp claws behind a tree,
Tasting blood everywhere,
Foxes growling and howling to the moon,
Spooky things popping up,
A mixture of monsters' heads staring at me
Finally got to a warm home at last.

Thomas Alcock (8)
Carmountside Primary School, Stoke-on-Trent

Night

Scary, terrifying footsteps,
Heard in the dark,
Owls hooting, staring out,
Tree branches cracking like skeletons,
Spooky eyes and torches shining on me,
Somebody's fingers touching me,
Feeling cold, lonely and terrified,
Tasting smoky fumes off cars,
Wind blowing me along the cold, damp floor,
Smelling black smoke,
Ah, seeing Christmas lights!
Home! I'm happy now.

Beth Cunningham (8)
Carmountside Primary School, Stoke-on-Trent

Night

Spooky lights like skeletons
In the dark, creepy footsteps,
Behind me wind pushing me along the damp road,
Trees bending ready to snap,
Foxes howling for food,
Dogs barking in the spooky streets,
Walls wobbling in the wind,
As I walk along,
Hooray!
I am home.

Jessica Hamilton (8)
Carmountside Primary School, Stoke-on-Trent

Night

Weird noises heard in the darkness
Tall trees look like giant skeletons
Tree claws cracking
Creepy, red eyes watching me
Seeing horror faces crowding around
Guitar sounds from Hell
Bottles smashing
Smelling fear in the damp, cold air
Scary, creepy sounds closer than ever
Markings on trees saying *die boy*
Finally the quiet night has come.

Jordan Simcock (8)
Carmountside Primary School, Stoke-on-Trent

Night

Creepy things all around me,
Spying on me,
Spooky trees crowding around me,
Foxes growling and staring at me,
Scared in case someone grabs me,
Fear is all around me,
Tree claws reaching on me,
Owls twisting their necks around,
All I heard was howling,
At last home with all my decorations!

Barry Jones (9)
Carmountside Primary School, Stoke-on-Trent

Night

Funky noises all around me,
Dogs and foxes howling for drink,
Scared eyes looking at me,
Smelling food and beer in the air,
Fumes in the air off vans and cars,
Trees crackling in the dark,
Footsteps following me on the path,
Feeling very scared and worried,
Branches touching my arms,
Bottles smashing on the road,
Finally, home and happy.

Craig Jones (9)
Carmountside Primary School, Stoke-on-Trent

Night

Scary footsteps,
Dogs and foxes howling at the moon,
Eyes watching me,
Shadows moving all around me,
Saggy wet clothes,
Splinters on my fingers from wood,
Tasting cold air
And smoke all around,
Smelling fumes kidnapping my nose,
Ah! Home at last!

Danica Craddock (8)
Carmountside Primary School, Stoke-on-Trent

Night

Wicked noises heard all around
Owls howling, birds creeping,
Footsteps squeaking,
Seeing weird lights
Shadows moving
Eyes watching me
Feels like branches touching me from all around
Wood cracking
Walls getting closer
Tasting cold air, smoke and fear
Smelling petrol fumes
Finally at home!

Luke Hoddle (9)
Carmountside Primary School, Stoke-on-Trent

Night

Creepy noises heard in the night,
Animals squeaking and trees creaking,
Footsteps stamping on the floor,
Seeing eyes, shadows and shapes,
Hedges rustling in the breeze,
Touching metal, wood and ground,
Tasting smoke and sweat,
Smelling fumes coming from cars
And animals too,
At last I see the light on in my house.

Naomi Baskerville (9)
Carmountside Primary School, Stoke-on-Trent

My Magic Box
(Based on 'Magic Box' by Kit Wright)

I will put in my box . . .
The sounds of the early morning birds calling at the beach,
The smells of the sea when walking along the beach at sunrise,
The taste of hot KFC going down my throat after the first bite,
The feel of shark and dolphin skin as you dive and swim with them,
The view of little children trying to run and play.

I will put in my box . . .
The sound of a puppy's claws on a wooden floor as he plays,
                                      it goes tip tap, tip tap,
The smell of lavender that makes your garden come alive,
The taste of chocolate going down my throat as I melt it in my mouth,
The feel of love for your family and friends,
The view of people having fun and laughing at all types of jokes.

I will put in my box . . .
The care I received from my family and friends,
My box is fashioned with love and care in the corners,
Inside I will put in my box my future dreams.

Rachel Meer (11)
Chaucer Junior School, Ilkeston

Chocolate

I eat so much chocolate, I drive my mum insane,
but I tell her not to worry, it's good for my brain.

I like chocolate, it tastes so very nice,
I like it so much, I have to eat it twice.

When I am down and feeling sad,
I have a bar of chocolate to make me feel glad.

Twix, Twirl and Mars
are my fave bars.

You can get chocolate mice
and they're much nicer than rice.

Emily Corns (8)
Chaucer Junior School, Ilkeston

Home From School

Seeing the coats swaying like the leaves on a tree
Seeing the television flickering like an old torch
Seeing half-open mail balancing on the edge of the table
Seeing the computer, still like an old postbox

Hearing next-door's cat miaowing quietly
Hearing cartoons on the TV upstairs in a mumbling sound
Hearing my mother chatting so fast the words come out blurred
Hearing a thumping noise of my brother getting home from school

Smelling the wonderful smell of dinner cooking
Smelling the faint smell of orange squash being poured
Smelling chocolate melting in my mouth
Smelling polish on the furniture

Tasting the salt from crisps on my tongue
Tasting orange squash, getting rid of my dry throat
Tasting melting chocolate oozing down my mouth
Tasting a single mint warming my mouth

Touching the keys on a keyboard sinking down
Touching the rough buttons on the remote control
Touching a cold glass making my fingers numb
Touching my book's pages turning.

Jason Blackman (9)
Chaucer Junior School, Ilkeston

People

She has long blonde hair and a piercing stare
She went to Hull and met a very big bull
She woke up and broke a cup
She went to The Deep but the stairs were too steep
Her name was Polly and she had a dolly
She went to Scarborough, they have a very big harbour
She wears black clothes and has hairy little toes
She had a dog called Maisy and she went very crazy
She had grey hair and a big stare.

Polly Love (8)
Chaucer Junior School, Ilkeston

Home From School

Seeing my rabbit running around like thunder,
Seeing my mum drinking a hot cup of coffee slowly,
Seeing a frothy cup of tea on the desk,
Seeing my homework staring at me,
Seeing the TV telling me to put it on,
Seeing a video being shown by my brother.

Hearing my brother playing on my black Game Cube,
Hearing my nana coughing badly,
Hearing my mum making a lovely cappuccino,
Hearing my brother turning up the sound on the TV,
Hearing my mum chattering fast to my nana.

Smelling my mum's home-made lovely chocolate sponge cakes,
Smelling my fish's tank like I'm right near it,
Smelling my brother's Lynx aftershave,
Smelling my mum's Warburton's crumpets.

Tasting my mum's big chocolate cake,
Tasting my mum's home-made pancakes,
Tasting what I'm having for tea,
Tasting my chocolate apple with chocolate sprinkles,
Tasting my M&Ms,
Tasting a McChicken Sandwich.

Touching a tin of Coke,
Touching the good TV,
Touching the wicked PS2,
Touching the cool Game Cube
Touching my felt tips
Touching my PS2 controls.

Jessé-Mae Breame (9)
Chaucer Junior School, Ilkeston

Friends

I've got some friends called Amy and Gemma.
Actually they're really quite clever!
I've also got a friend called Daisy,
But don't think about calling her lazy!
I've got a boyfriend called Richard
And he doesn't like to be pictured.
Along with all of them I've got my mate Josh,
He's very, very posh!
There's Ewa who likes to play on the Sims,
She's really glad she's got 4 limbs!
There's also Shauna,
Whose worst enemy's name is Dorna!
Last of all there's my best friend, Charlotte,
Who when she's embarrassed, goes bright scarlet!

Isabella Hawkes (8)
Chaucer Junior School, Ilkeston

Home From School

Seeing the dog prance around ruining stuff
Seeing the rabbit munching the lovely marigolds

Hearing my sister and brother scrapping and scratching
Hearing my dad and me doing the belly button band and my dog
doing the band too

Smelling the fabulous food steaming
Smelling my sister's grubby feet

Tasting orange sliding down
Tasting my fabulous food

Touching the numbers on the alarm
Touching the garden fork ready to garden.

Aaron Brown (9)
Chaucer Junior School, Ilkeston

Home From School

Seeing my dog Charlie sunbathing in the sunny weather,
Seeing my friends walking home talking as their voices
travel through the air
Seeing my fish swimming in their home with happiness
Seeing my friends running around calling for me

Hearing the filter in the fish tank bubbling as my fish swim about
Hearing my friends knocking on the door as I dawdle because
I do not want to play
Hearing the gate suddenly shaking as I walk through
Hearing my friends' voices hollow through my house

Smelling the pork dinner as my mother cooks it
Smelling my friends' disgusting socks stinking in my house
Smelling the dog's hairs where he's been lounging on the settee
Smelling the polished house as my mum polishes it again

Tasting the fresh air wave into my mouth
Tasting the sandwich softening in my mouth
Tasting the crispy crisps in my mouth
Tasting the comfy cake, that soft you could sleep on it.

Loui Watson (8)
Chaucer Junior School, Ilkeston

Forest Animals

The squirrel is brown
And it jumps up and down
There's a singing bird
I'm surprised you haven't heard
I saw a frog
It was sitting on a log
I was eating a pea
Then I saw a big bee
A very big bear
Has a lot of hair
There's a wolf down there
It's chasing a hare.

James Harrison (8)
Chaucer Junior School, Ilkeston

Hunting

While lions are sleeping,
There's a hunter creeping
Around for tigers in the grass,
For every animal in the jungle fears him to pass.

The hunter has a weapon,
This weapon is a gun,
All the poor animals scatter and run,
Surely for the animals this is no fun.

When a baby elephant
Gets separated from its mum
Or when an innocent little monkey
Gets put in a cage.

Mothers full of rage,
Animals have fears,
They also have tears.

Jade Scarborough (10)
Chaucer Junior School, Ilkeston

Bones

I found a bone and took it home
I dug a hole and frightened a mole
I put it in a ditch
I hope that little robin that saw me doesn't snitch
I covered it with muck and I hope I have some luck
I woke up in the morning
It was so early it was still dawning.

Peta Brown (8)
Chaucer Junior School, Ilkeston

Home From School

Seeing my brother watching TV,
Seeing my cats eating,
Seeing my dinner get put out.

Hearing my front door creaking,
Hearing my mum shouting as they eat tea.

Smelling my delightful dinner cooking,
Smelling my cats' food as they eat,
Smelling my dog's food.

Tasting my dinner as it cooks,
Tasting my drink when we are at the table.

Touching my bike to go to the park,
Touching my clothes when I get changed.

Byron Fitchett (8)
Chaucer Junior School, Ilkeston

Home From School

Seeing my mum turn the keys in the lock,
Seeing my dog's tear and chomp at their food,
Seeing my mum getting stressed out over the dinner.

Hearing the stair-gate squeak open,
Hearing the digger dig near the window.

Smelling the beef bits in my pot noodle,
Smelling the freshness of my mum's fresh perfume.

Tasting the truffle chocolates after my tea,
Tasting the saltiness in my bag of crisps.

Touching the remote control as I change the channels,
Touching my fork as I dig into my dinner.

Kay Mather (9)
Chaucer Junior School, Ilkeston

Home From School

Seeing my mum and dad cook happily together as I sit down
to read my school books
Seeing my dog sitting on the sofa as if she is waiting for
me to come home
She waits for an hour
Seeing the TV as I begin to turn it on
With the prickly remote control to watch CITV
Seeing my room as my mum helps to clean it

Hearing the TV because I am relaxing after school
Hearing a conversation on the telephone in the kitchen
Hearing my 14-year-old brother moan about his day
Hearing my dog whine for nice food at teatime

Smelling my brother's horrible smelly feet
Smelling my grandma's home as I walk through the door from school
Smelling the air as I walk to my grandma's

Tasting a nice hot cup of tea
Tasting the salty crisps as I plunged them into my mouth
Tasting the ice cream after my tea
Tasting a nice hot cup of cocoa before I do my homework

Touching the door as I walk through
Touching my TV as my brother Dan got an episode of Charmed
Touching the telephone as I phone my mates
Touching my CD player as I put Westlife on to dance to.

Louise Draper (9)
Chaucer Junior School, Ilkeston

Euro 2004

David Beckham,
Paul Scholes,
We are going
To score lots of goals

Zidane, Rooney,
Raul, bravo
We're going to win 8-0, bravo!
We're going to win 8-0, bravo!

Portugal, England,
France and Germany,
Some of the best teams in the land,
Let's all hope none of them get banned.

Fans booing,
Players shooting,
Flying tackles,
High-pitched cackles.

Thomas Robinson (10)
Chaucer Junior School, Ilkeston

Euro 2004

E uropean teams,
U niting teams together,
R ehearsing is over,
O n the sixth month the most important cup ever to be won

2 top teams in for the chance of a lifetime
0 more chances
0 going back
4 teams in a group to get in the final.

Ben Massey (9)
Chaucer Junior School, Ilkeston

Home From School

Seeing my cat Jonsey jumping down the stairs,
Seeing the plain white door that leads into the lounge,
Seeing a little black figure behind the banister of the stairs.

Hearing the sizzling sound of the metal cooker cooking my food,
Hearing Jonsey purring loudly around my leg,
Hearing the little black figure, Conan, miaowing in a squeaky voice in
the background,
Hearing my brother's music on full blast.

Smelling my mum's wonderful cooking,
Smelling the sweet aroma of a plant,
Smelling the beautiful cut hedges in the garden.

Tasting my mum's beautiful cooking,
Tasting the lovely fresh fruit out of the fridge,
Tasting the clear cool water out of the filter in the fridge
Tasting the chocolaty taste of a cookie

Touching the smooth kitchen top
Touching the jar of cookies
Touching the smooth handle of the wooden door.

Samuel Jones (9)
Chaucer Junior School, Ilkeston

Animals!

Tortoises moving slowly around,
Little feet plodding on the ground,
Turtles sitting at the bottom of the sea,
Eating their yummy tea,
Creepy-crawlies playing hide-and-seek,
So don't peek,
Now the wiggly worms begin to sleep,
With creepy-crawlies above their feet.

Natasha Williams (10)
Chaucer Junior School, Ilkeston

My Pet Problem

Animals are great,
They're like your best mate,
I've got a few of my own,
Living in my home,
My dog has a bone,
My cat has a mat,
My horse has some hay,
The puppy's caught the cat!

My bird's got some seeds,
My rabbit's eating the weeds,
My hamster's cheeks are going to pop!
But what about the dwarf lop?
He's cuddly,
He's cute,
The cockerel goes *hoot! hoot!*
All the animals in my house are fluffy,
Cute and cuddly,
When it comes to the vet bill,
I'm searching for my money.

Alexandra Beviss (9)
Chaucer Junior School, Ilkeston

My Little Ladybird

My little ladybird
So round and small,
It pats its little feet
As it crawls.

Then it flies
Up high
And its spots
Twinkle in the sky.

Nada Baker (10)
Chaucer Junior School, Ilkeston

Monkeys In The Jungle

M onkeys in the trees
O pening bananas
N aughty as can be
K ings of the jungle that's what they ought to be
E ating bananas as many as they can fit in their belly
Y awning at night, energetic in the morning
S winging through the jungle, branch to branch

I n and out the trees, scaring all the bees
N osy-parkers, that's what they are

T rees are monkeys' favourite things to climb
H anging onto branches having lots of fun
E ating bananas all around the world

J umping up and down
U p and down, giving everyone a fright
N aughty monkeys playing in mud
G oing to climb trees I guess
L ong arms, short arms and legs, monkeys all have them
E ating other monkeys, that's what they do sometimes.

Chloe Crawshaw (10)
Chaucer Junior School, Ilkeston

World War Two

W althers firing
O verhead bombers
R ed leaking from bodies
L ives being lost from both sides
D emolition charges

W orld domination
A nti aircraft guns
R aids from Germans

T hompsons killing people
W ar-torn countries
O ver 10,000 dead.

Kyran Deakin (10)
Chaucer Junior School, Ilkeston

Haunted House

In the woods is a castle
With slamming doors,
but no one's there
That sounds the creaking floor.

Falling plates,
Breaking chairs,
There is over
A thousand stairs,

Upon the hill
Is a black cat,
It's the servant,
It wears a top hat.

It's got red eyes
And a long thin tail,
It only weighs,
One stone on the scale.

Howls in the night,
That sends a shiver
Down your spine,
It cracks the windows,
They're very fine.

There's a wizard in the cellar,
He brews spells,
To kill
Aunt Bella!

Jacob Robinson (10)
Chaucer Junior School, Ilkeston

The War

There's buckets of blood,
Falling in the mud,
As the sword went through his heart!
He's not that smart,
He's not that smart.

There's an axe in his back,
His spine starts to crack,
The German commander stood on his head
And now he's dead
And now he's dead.

Commander Smith
Slipped off a cliff,
He landed in the Trojan War,
His body got torn,
His body got torn.

There was one man
That shot at a van,
Everybody that's inside
They nearly died,
They nearly died.

Their last defence
Was to break down the fence,
He used a gun and shot Commander Ron
And now he's gone
And now he's gone.

Sergeant Fred,
Shot a German in the head,
Now the war is all done,
They can all have fun,
They can all have fun.

Brendon Limb (9)
Chaucer Junior School, Ilkeston

My Magic Box
(Based on 'Magic Box' by Kit Wright)

I will put in my box . . .
The sounds of early birds
Singing in the branches,
The smell of freshly baked bread
As it cools ready for me to eat,
The taste of melted chocolate in my mouth melting
The feel of soft rabbit's fur as I softly stroke it,
The view of the sunset at the eve of the day.

I will put in my box . . .
The sound of a baby laughing out loud at people,
The smell of a scented gel pen as I am writing,
The taste of ice cream when in my mouth,
The feel of a baby's skin so smooth and gentle,
The view of a rainy day when no one's out.

I will put in my box . . .
My wish for a grade in my SATs results,
My box is fashioned with teardrops
And rays of the sun sparkling.

Carmel Eyre (11)
Chaucer Junior School, Ilkeston

Animals

A is for amazing ants crawling everywhere
N is for nasty tigers striking for their prey
I is for insects some flying, some jumping and some crawling
M is for mad monkeys jumping from tree to tree
A is for a weird anteater eating ants from every hole
L is for loyal lions fighting for their pack
S is for slippery snakes that slide through the grass.

Shelby Boyles (10)
Chaucer Junior School, Ilkeston

Millennium Stadium

At the Millennium Stadium the match begins
For a spot in the Champions League
Man United
Man United
This crucial game will be very fast
Hopefully we will win the present like in the past
Man United
Man United
Ronaldo breaks the deadlock with a beautiful strike
Millwall's near goal puts the fans in fright
Man United
Man United
Millwall nearly score again, it's not looking good
Nistelrooy puts it 2-0 up with a beautiful penalty
Man United
Man United
The final whistle goes just after Nistelrooy scores
A penalty shoot-out is not needed after all
Man United
Man United.

Jake Dean (10)
Chaucer Junior School, Ilkeston

Euro 2004

E ngland go into the final
N ever will they go down
G oal three for Owen!
L osing will be terrible
A ll the fans go wild
N eville defending the ball
D avid Beckham crossing it in from the wing.

Cameron Scarle (10)
Chaucer Junior School, Ilkeston

Dragons Flying

D ragons flying in the air
R ipping open the king of hair
A ngrily destroying a town
G rabbing his dressing gown
O n his personal tour
N aughty as can be
S tupidity

F loating in the sky
L icking his lips
Y ellow eyes like the moon
I n the sky so silently
N ot ready for his tea
G oing to bed at 12am.

Louis Clegg (10)
Chaucer Junior School, Ilkeston

What Am I?

My ears are floppy
I am fluffy and cuddly
I love carrots
They are the best!
Cabbages and lettuce, yummy!
I can hop, jump, skip all day long,
I live in a hutch,
With lots of space,
My claws are small and sharp,
I am very bouncy,
My tail is a ball of cotton.
I bet you can guess
What I am . . .

Ellie Bednall (10)
Chaucer Junior School, Ilkeston

My Magic Box

(Based on 'Magic Box' by Kit Wright)

I will put in my box . . .
The sounds of a wave flowing into the caves
The smell of flowers in a field for all to see
The taste of hot chocolate on a cold night
The feel of a cold surface on a hot day
The view of a kitten playing with some cotton

I will put in my box . . .
The sounds of a cricket in the night
The smell of a fish and chip shop at the beach
The taste of melon on a hot day
The feel of the water splashing in your face on the rapids
The view of a newborn puppy that walks around lost

I will put in my box . . .
The Manchester football team winning the Premiership

My box is fashioned with pictures of my friends and gold coins
In the corners are my family

I will put in my best friends who I can trust.

Jack Andrews (11)
Chaucer Junior School, Ilkeston

Euro 2004

E uropean football team fans flow in the crowd like clouds in the sky
U nited football teams winning and losing, they won't give up
R eds, blues, whites and blacks, what is your team?
O ut in the stadium fans forever seen.

Jamie Chaplin (10)
Chaucer Junior School, Ilkeston

Haunted House

I live in a house,
A house that has a mouse,
Now that mouse is being chased by a lizard,
That lizard belonged to a wizard,
The wizard saw a ghost,
A ghost that was a TV host,
The ghost had a friend mummy,
The mummy had a dummy,
The dummy was used by a baby zombie
And killing was his favourite hobby,
Now I can see a vampire,
He looks as if he's on fire,
Now I can see a skeleton,
Sitting next to a Wellington,
The skeleton is alive
And through a beehive,
It plays tennis,
It's a menace,
My mum and dad are dead
And they both chopped off my brother's head,
His head rolled on the floor,
It rolled out of the front door,
Instead of having a head,
He had a beehive instead,
The mouse has a fright,
When it strikes midnight,
A werewolf creeps behind me
And he rips the zombies apart and hands me my key,
The werewolf is my friend.

Daniel Briggs (9)
Chaucer Junior School, Ilkeston

Haunted House

When it's 9 o'clock and I'm snug in bed
I feel something under my head
I know it's a feather poking at me
Sometimes it tickles me *tee hee!*
And it makes me queasy because the air's cold
And down at the graveyard they break the mould
And that's what happens when I'm tucked up in bed
And they are the living dead
They pull my covers from me
They shout my name, 'Lee! Lee!'
Into another room I go
That's where I hide low
I'm crying, I believe I'm dying!
I whisper to myself, *'It's time to pray'*
I went into the garden where Max lay
It's really hard to concentrate
When you're being chased by dreaded hate
Go back in the house and up the stairs
Now they're roaring like grizzly bears
I start to face them bravely alone
But at that moment the bell rang on the phone
The ghouls ran away as fast as they could
One of them slipped on the coat with the hood
I picked up the phone, there was no one there!
But then something really gave me a scare
It was a vampire on the phone
Just then I remembered I'm home alone
It was a vampire on the phone!
He smashed down the door, it was in bits on the floor
I said to myself, *'Mum's gonna kill me for this'*
Then he gave me a great big *hissss*
I escaped to the roof in the middle of the night
That gave me a fright

I found two sticks, I put them into a cross
The vampire looked, he slipped on some moss
He rolled down the roof and onto a fence
I thought, *oh gosh that must be intense*
I fled to my room and fell sound asleep
In the morning, '*Cock-a-doodle-do*' called the hen
Tonight the nightmare will begin again.

Joshua Price (10)
Chaucer Junior School, Ilkeston

My Magic Box
(Based on 'Magic Box' by Kit Wright)

I will put in my box . . .
The sounds of waves crashing up against rocky cliffs
The smell of Big Macs as I strolled past McDonald's
on a frosty morning
The taste of strawberries and cream as I eat my dessert
The feel of a freshly-made bed as I slowly sink into it
The view of countryside filled with lovely flowers

I will put in my box . . .
The sound of whales calling to each other under the open ocean
The smell of bacon as I pass the kitchen on the way to school
The taste of chocolate as I eat the scrumptious treat
The feel of my cat's fur as she rubs up against my legs
The view of horses prancing and dancing in an empty field

I will put in my box . . .
Photos of my treasured horses in Ireland
Dolphins diving beneath the deep wide ocean
My baby cousin's first smile
The sunrise as I slowly go down the street

My box is fashioned in
Horse pictures and the corners are filled with horse saddles
The hinges are from steel horseshoes.

Christina Jackson (11)
Chaucer Junior School, Ilkeston

Haunted House!

There was a haunted house
And there throughout a vampire's lair,
Were acid and bombs,
Which the vampire did not care.

A hundred years within,
The house was sold,
In there were bodies, dead and cold,
In came a man
Who liked his house spick and span
And then one night,
The man could hear
Voices in the closet near.

There was creeping and shrieking,
Under the floor,
He found three ghosts and a vampire
Opening the door.

The haunted house is still there this day,
Which belongs to three ghosts and a vampire they say,
No one knows what happened to the man,
The four still live there to this day!

Laurie Trueman (10)
Chaucer Junior School, Ilkeston

Euro 2004

E ngland are to win the golden cup
U K should cheer for them and pray to win
R ounding down the bad scores for France
O ur Owen will score a goal for the team in the back of the net.

2 goals from Becks!
0 goals from Owen!
0 goals from Scholes!
4 goals from England!

Sean Green (10)
Chaucer Junior School, Ilkeston

My Magic Box

(Based on 'Magic Box' by Kit Wright)

I will put in my box . . .
The sound of the sea crashing amongst the rocks,
The smell of a Big Mac being eaten by me,
The taste of ice cream soothing my frozen tongue,
The feel of silk sliding through my fingers,
The view of the clouds gliding past.

I will put in my box . . .
The sound of dance music beating through my ears,
The smell of sweet candyfloss wafting past me,
The taste of chicken being squashed by my teeth,
The feel of foam tickling my hand,
The view of fire blazing in the air.

I will put in my box . . .
The proudness of when I achieve my fame,
The greatness of winning a competition,
The thrill of excitement and good news.

My box is fashioned with
The beat of music in the lock,
The sparkle of the stars on the lid
And in the corners are happy memories.

I will put in my box . . .
The gift of life and the winds of change.

Jack Hallam (11)
Chaucer Junior School, Ilkeston

War

W orld domination
A ir bombing
R uthless killing.

Jamie Gingell (10)
Chaucer Junior School, Ilkeston

Different Things!

A cat in a box,
Sat next to a fox,
The shoes are walking,
The women are talking,
Children are smiling,
While teachers are filing,
Big boys playing,
While men are scoring,
The war is fighting,
With people crowding,
The Queen is sitting,
While men are standing,
Trees growing,
Leaves falling,
Lying in bed,
While others may be dying,
The light bulb glows,
While the wind blows,
The birds singing,
While others are flying,
Big trees,
With branches dropping,
Birds flying.

Jessica Frost (10)
Chaucer Junior School, Ilkeston

Euro 2004

E ngland will win, will beat all the rest
U nited, supporters cheer England on
R oaring crowds cheer the goals
O wen will help us on the way to win
  Euro 2004.

Elliot Johnson (10)
Chaucer Junior School, Ilkeston

The Spooky Dooky Haunted House

There is a phantom creeping around
As the ghostly party begins
I can hear stealthy footsteps in the shadows
Creak! Crack!
I feel the house is quivering
I better hide in the cobwebbed cupboard
Oh no! Oh no! It is that creaking floorboard again
I'm feeling crinkly fingers tickling me
I better watch out
My teeth begin to chatter
I hear another ghost snoring, 'S*h! sh!'*
Don't want to wake him
I think I'd better get out of this place
Did you hear that noise?

Louise Smith (10)
Chaucer Junior School, Ilkeston

Home From School

Seeing a red checked dress lying on a fold-out chair
Seeing the big red patterned sofa as I relax on it
Seeing the silver pacific TV as I watch Hollyoaks
Seeing the green garden with unused toys

Hearing the loud TV as I watch CBBC
Hearing my mum coughing as she was doing some work
Hearing my brother shouting at Mum as loud as a foghorn
Hearing my brother's trains as they run across the track

Smelling my mum smoking as the cigarette burns
Smelling my salt and vinegar crisps as I smell them
Smelling my mum eating hot pasta with pasta sauce.

Paige Bradshaw (9)
Chaucer Junior School, Ilkeston

Home From School

Seeing my dog looking at me turning his smooth head timidly
Seeing my mum changing channels on the TV
Seeing the dark green couch against the wall
Seeing the creaky cupboard as I take my coat off

Hearing my dog running towards me
Getting his claws stuck in the carpet
Hearing my mum shouting angrily at the dog
Hearing the kettle boiling the cold water
Hearing the telly blasting out at full volume

Smelling the dinner cooking in the white gas oven
Smelling the fruity air freshener blowing in the lounge
Smelling my mum's perfume whiffing around the house

Tasting my cheese and onion crisps crunching in my mouth.

Sam Tuck (9)
Chaucer Junior School, Ilkeston

War

Things are blown up by tanks
Things like sheds made of planks
War is bad for the world
A person had a knife in them and curled
Tanks are the best weapons to use
Some people die from abuse
Oh war, oh war, oh war
People do not adore
The worst war of all is a civil war
The rulers of the world want more.

Connor Page (10)
Chaucer Junior School, Ilkeston

Home From School

Seeing my cute dog jumping on everyone as they walk in
Seeing my mice scratch me because it hurts and they're excited to see
me
Seeing my candle in my bedroom flicker slowly in the dark

Hearing my mice in the cage rattling as if they're glad to see me back
from school
Hearing a sound of the swing as it squeaks like a mother mouse

Smelling my grandma's Smartie biscuits in the oven
They smell like a chef's toffee ice cream
Smelling my flowers in the garden as yellow as can be

Tasting my salt and vinegar crisps that make me sneeze
Also makes my mouth go all tingly like an electric shock
Tasting the paint dry in the white and orange hallway
Tasting the chocolate bubbling in my mouth like great big bubbles
someone's blowing

Touching my clothes blowing in the wind
Touching my lolly that freezes my teeth
Touching my cup of tea that I made
Touching my mice as I walk in
Touching my microphone doing karaoke.

Rebecca Heywood (8)
Chaucer Junior School, Ilkeston

Dolphins

Diving dolphin in the deep blue sea,
Flipper is his name, he's a friend of me,
He swims all day and sleeps all night
And sometimes catches a fish to bite,
He likes to play and prance around,
A better friend I have never found,
He's a friend, I love him dear,
I always like to keep him near.

Ellie Thompson (10)
Chaucer Junior School, Ilkeston

Euro 2004 England

E ngland rock the world
U K shall win all games
R umble 'cause England is coming home
O ur Beckham curves a ball, *wow! Wow!*

2 goals from Rooney
0 goals from Scholes
0 goals from Gary Neville
4 goals from Owen

E ngland are the best of the west
N ever will they lose for England
G etting ready for France to come to England
L eicester City don't score past David James
A ll the people support you, England!
N ever, never, never will they lose, England!
D avid James saves again.

Ben Connelly (10)
Chaucer Junior School, Ilkeston

Home From School

Seeing my garden growing
Seeing the dinner on the table

Hearing dogs barking
Hearing my dinner bubbling

Smelling my lovely air-freshener
Smelling my fish
Smelling my lovely dinner

Tasting my lovely Pot Noodle
Tasting the lovely juice running down my neck
Tasting the lovely sauce

Touching the loud telly
Touching my mum
Touching my dad.

Scott Eyre (9)
Chaucer Junior School, Ilkeston

Home From School

Seeing my dog trying to run off as fast as lightning,
Seeing my cat running outside to fight with other cats,
Seeing my brother playing on his PlayStation trying to complete levels.

Hearing my dog on her lead all ready to go for a walk
To go and run off and chase birds,
Hearing my cat wanting his food, waiting very patiently.

Smelling the dinner cooking as fast as it can,
Smelling the toast smothering with smoke,
Smelling the dog's dinner with runny gravy,
Smelling the dog when she's been in the rain.

Tasting the things in my room with perfume,
Tasting the dinner cooking and garlic bread with very nice spices,
Tasting my lovely iced pop put in the freezer,
Tasting my perfume and air freshener in my room.

Touching the wardrobe to get my clothes to go outside,
Touching the dog and cat because they have got wet from outside
Touching the cupboard drawers to get the food that I really like.

Kirsty Nadin (9)
Chaucer Junior School, Ilkeston

Slithering Snake

S limy snakes slithering through tall spiky grass
N ever let go of their prey
A lways their scales shimmer in the golden sun
K illing their prey with their threatening fangs
E very day watch out for slimy snakes.

Marcus Woollands (10)
Chaucer Junior School, Ilkeston

Home From School

Seeing the telephone on top of the extremely scruffy phone books,
Seeing the pine table with all the clean knifes and forks all
ready for tea,
Seeing the garden plants which are beautiful pink roses.

Hearing the cat purring all curled in his fluffy bed,
Hearing my sister crying because she had just tripped over
a bumpy stone,
Hearing my cat jumping out of his bed miaowing a high-pitched
sound for his food.

Smelling the fresh air as it sways past my nose,
Smelling the chips coming out of the oven all crispy and thick,
Smelling the orange peel going into the bin because my sister
has just finished it.

Alice Macqueen (9)
Chaucer Junior School, Ilkeston

Home From School

Seeing my mum cooking my tea in the kitchen over the oven
Seeing the CITV programme on the telly making noises
Seeing my brother's arguing loudly upstairs
Seeing myself sinking into the settee

Hearing my music playing so loudly like an aeroplane crashing
Hearing my brothers Xbox roaring on wrestling
Hearing the telly talking about yucky stuff
Hearing my mum talk about school to Ricky

Smelling the cakes freshly baked that smell sweet
Smelling the pie being made that's great
Smelling the sour lemon from the fruit bowl
Smelling my mum's flower perfume from the lounge.

Kelly Barker (8)
Chaucer Junior School, Ilkeston

Home From School

Touching the comfy chair,
Touching the hairy hamster,
Touching my barking dogs, Checker and Samson

Seeing the loud TV
Seeing my quiet brother sleeping
Seeing the big brown sofa

Hearing the TV on loud
Hearing my uncle shout at the dogs
Hearing the cooker bubble

Smelling the warm dinner cooking
Smelling the warm curry and rice

Tasting the hot curry and rice
Tasting the chocolate slipping down my throat.

Courtney Reeve (8)
Chaucer Junior School, Ilkeston

Home From School

Seeing my beautiful sweet coffee as white as the clouds drifting by
Seeing my lovely sugary biscuits round like a ball
Seeing my beautiful widescreen TV as wide as a digger
Seeing my dad's dozy, sleepy eyes rolling like balls

Hearing loud annoying music made by Connor louder
                              than a jack hammer
Hearing my dad shouting as loud as he can

Smelling horrible eggs as smelly as poo
Smelling sweet coffee as smelly as perfume.

Stefan May (9)
Chaucer Junior School, Ilkeston

Home From School

Seeing my guinea pigs scuttling about like a roller coaster,
Going around and around, scared that someone will come
                                        and stamp on them,
Seeing myself in the mirror just standing there as if I had been frozen,
Seeing the furry cover on the sofa, so soft that it could be a
                                        very cuddly animal,
Seeing my school work face to face with me,
So close to me is was like a sticky custard pie being thrown at me.

Hearing the big TV blabbering on about boring stuff,
So annoying you could chuck a brick at it,
Hearing the cat miaowing at the door thinking how to get out
                                        of this silly and stupid place,
Hearing my friends jiggering and rambling on as they play,
Hearing my dog barking as I enter the booming and banging house!

Smelling my tea cooking in the fiery oven,
Smelling my dog's bad breath as he walks past very slowly
                                        and it follows him everywhere he goes,
Smelling the scent of the gorgeous soap as I wash my dirty hands,
Smelling a pot of pourri as smelly as a proper rose in a vase
And it feels like it's going to smell forever!

Lauren Roberts (9)
Chaucer Junior School, Ilkeston

A Humorous Pet Shop Poem

From the pet shop I would like . . .
A slimy, slithery snake
That likes to eat cake,
A dancing diamond dog
That likes to eat logs,
A clever, crazy cat
That likes to get fat,
A black, bouncy bear
That likes to sit on a chair.

Brendan Gough (7)
Chaucer Junior School, Ilkeston

Home From School

Seeing the dog galloping right round the lawn before eating her
scrumptious doggie drops
Seeing the TV crackling away with static electricity as I
watch football on video
Seeing the garden as I play volleyball over the fence with next door
Seeing the conservatory as light glistens through the windows
As I rest on the squidgy settee

Hearing the dog as she eats her smelly dinner
Hearing the noisy children next door playing with a ball
Hearing the clock ticking away as tea approaches
Hearing my sister squealing at the top of her voice

Smelling the flowers as I played football
Smelling my cheese and tomato pizza cooking, perfuming the air
Smelling my sister eating Quavers and making everywhere smell
Smelling air freshener tingling up the top of my nose

Tasting the Coke bubbling up my nose and making me sneeze.

Jake Ledger (9)
Chaucer Junior School, Ilkeston

The Haunted House

H aunted house,
A ll the spiders
U nder the floorboards,
N ext to the door,
T hink of the smell,
E ek, eek goes the stairs as you walk,
D angerous witches cackling.

H iding bats on the ceiling,
O ut run all the children,
U nusual faces appear at night,
S piders crawling up the walls,
E very little child has disappeared.

Kayleigh Waller (10)
Chaucer Junior School, Ilkeston

War

At sad places all the children shoot for their lives,
Jet planes scream through the sky,
Homes of the gun-less smashed and burned,
Peace smashed into 1000 pieces,
No one knows when they will die,
Everyone knows they will.

The windows get bashed,
All the people get scared,
You are always hearing guns,
When all the dads go to peaceful countries with their sons
And all the mothers go to peaceful countries,
No one goes to school or work,
No more life around,
Only big bangs, no fun,
Yes! The war is over, no more dying, no more crying.

Daniel Gale (9)
Chaucer Junior School, Ilkeston

Haunted House

Higher and higher
It gets scarier

At the house is a nasty ghost

Under the creaky floor
Are mice and rats

Now the lock is moving by
Ghosts trying to get in

Try to get out if you can

Howling and screeching from the attic
And the cellar, there's ghosts everywhere

Down in the basement
There's rats, cats, and loads of bats.

Jordan Green (10)
Chaucer Junior School, Ilkeston

Home From School

Seeing my mum cooking tea, it is delicious,
Seeing my lovely telly and my incy wincy Game Cube,
Seeing my big England bed in front of me when I am in my room,
Seeing the cooker as my mum is cooking the delicious tea.

Hearing my mum bellowing at my big brother because he
                              gets a bad report every day,
Hearing the loud whistling kettle because my mum is
                              always making cups of tea,
Hearing my next-door neighbour's cat miaowing quietly,
Hearing CBBC on the TV that is very loud.

Smelling the gorgeous cup of tea that my mum is gulping down,
Smelling my lovely tea being made,
Smelling the next-door neighbour's cat's poo
Smelling ashes from cigarettes outside.

Dale Nind (8)
Chaucer Junior School, Ilkeston

Haunted House

H aunted house all old and creaky,
A ghost and a vampire make my hair go all freaky,
U nicorns are dreams,
N ightmares are always a haunted house and their schemes,
T he haunted house tears me out of my skin,
E erie creaky floorboards are very, very thin,
D readful things happen in the haunted house.

H aunted house has a terrible mouse,
O w, bang, ow, ow, bang, ow,
U gly monsters and the Grim Reaper,
S melly mummies in a case, guarded by a long dead housekeeper,
E rr, bang, ow, err, bang, ow.

Cannon Oakley-Thorpe (9)
Chaucer Junior School, Ilkeston

My Magic Box

(Based on 'Magic Box' by Kit Wright)

I will put in my box . . .
The sound of a dolphin swimming through the fresh ocean
water calling for attention
The smell of candyfloss tickling my nose
The taste of an ice cream on a hot summer's day
The feel of a silk wedding dress hanging up in a shop
The view of an ocean from the cliff top

I will put in my box . . .
The sound of the theme tune to my favourite show
The smell of talcum powder from a freshly changed baby
The taste of sour candy making me pull faces
The feel of a wet dolphin at the edge of the pool
The view of a litter of newborn puppies

I will put in my box . . .
Liverpool winning the FA Cup
My box is fashioned with everything I have inside my box
With the lid decorated with a bottlenose dolphin
leaping out of the Pacific Ocean
Inside the corners I will put golden varnished metal to make it look
even more special.

Hannah Heywood (10)
Chaucer Junior School, Ilkeston

Farm Animals

Hickerty horses trotting around
They normally end with a slip on the ground

Cowardly cows running away
You ought to sell one and get your pay

Challenging chickens take flying lessons
And some of the best make good impressions.

Joe Taylor (8)
Chaucer Junior School, Ilkeston

My Teacher

My teacher is as light as rain
But sometimes she can be a pain
Her name is Miss Sawyer
And she was a lawyer
She likes to have a flight
Sometimes a bike
She's as thin as a pin
And has a very big bin
She likes to go shopping
And eats cake toppings
She has golden hair
And doesn't play fair
She yells like a preacher
Yes, that's my teacher.

Katie Meer (8)
Chaucer Junior School, Ilkeston

Home From School

Seeing the door when I get in for home
Seeing I am watching TV when I am at home
Seeing the hot, hot food in my belly

Hearing the loud TV when I was with my dad's stinky feet
Hearing my grandad snoring loudly

Touching the car's ice-cool door handle
Touching my special dog and cat and dad and mum and sitter

Tasting the chips and big fish
Tasting the best cake in the world

Smelling the hot, hot food
Smelling the dog and cat and mum and dad and sitter.

Ben French (9)
Chaucer Junior School, Ilkeston

Letter Alphabet

A is for Abby who always comes first,
B is or Ben who is always the worst,
C is for Curtis who smells like cheese,
D is for Darren who never says please,
E is for Emily who always eats fast,
F is for Frank who is always last,
G is for Georgina who is really mean,
H is for Hannah who is a drama queen,
I is for Ian who always tells lies,
J is for Jack who ate all the pies,
K is for Karen who is always sick,
L is for Laura who fancies Nick
M is for Max whose dad owns a Boro
N is for Nick who fancies Laura
O is for Odie who loves football
P is for Peter who is very tall
Q is for Quinn who plays all the time
R is for Rhian who can never rhyme
S is for Stacey who made these words
T is for Tanya who shoots all the birds
U is for Uirian who is very spotty
V is for Victoria who is quite snotty
W is for Will who is always scared
X is for Xander who is always dared
Y is for Yuna who never says yes
Z is for Zack who is always the best!

Stacey Ellis (11)
Coten End Primary School, Warwick

The People In My Class

A is for Abbey who's really neat
B is for Ben who's got muddy feet,
C is for Cameron who's always in a stress,
D is for Danielle who hates to wear a dress,
E is for Ed who has a silly head
F is for Fred who likes to lay in his bed
G is for Georgina who looks up high
H is for Hannah who says goodbye
I is for Isabel who likes to write
J is for Joshua who's really bright
K is for Kim who calls her doll Poppy
L is for Lucy who likes to lick a lolly
M is for Martin who's a matchmaker
N is for Nick who's a baker
O is for Oliver who likes to eat
P is for Paul who hates meat
Q is for Quinn who can make a door
R is for Rebecca who is quite poor
S is for Stacey who has ginger hair
T is for Tanya who likes to share
U is for Una who is the person who has lots of pens
V is for Val who is always in with the hens
W is for Will who hates to pay
X is for Xander who's into rays
Y is for Yeovil who loves to sit by the tree
Z is for Zena who hates bees.

Emma O'Dwyer (10)
Coten End Primary School, Warwick

Lord Of The Rings Poem

A is for Aragorn, king of Gondor,
B is for Boromir who got killed,
C is for catapult, in battles,
D is for dwarves in Balin's tomb,
E is for Eowyn the princess of Rohan,
F is for Faramir the prince of Gondor,
G is for Gondor, the white city and Gandalf
                           and Gimli the dwarf,
H is for Horfax, the king of the horses,
I is for Isengard, the tower of Saruman,
J is for jousting in Rohan,
K is for the Keep in Helm's Deep,
L is for Legolas, the prince of Lothive,
M is for Minas Tirith, the place in Gondor
               and Mordor, the place where Sauron lived,
N is for Nazgul that a ringwraith rides on,
O is for Uruk-hai where Saruman lives,
P is for Pelinor fields outside Gondor,
Q is for Quiton in Middle Earth,
R is for Rohan, where Eowyn lives,
S is for Sauron and Saruman,
T is for troll, who nearly killed Aragorn,
U is for Uruk-hai, in the battle for Helm's Deep,
V is for victory,
W is for war,
X is for x-tra power for Gandalf,
Y is for the year, of the year of Gondor,
Z is for zapped by Gandalf, the white wizard.

James Gillett (11)
Coten End Primary School, Warwick

Colours

What is blue?
Water is blue.

What is red?
Blood is red.

What is green?
Leaves are green.

What is yellow?
Sand is yellow.

What is orange?
Oranges are orange.

What is pink?
Blossom is pink.

What is black?
Darkness is black.

What is white?
Light is white.

What is brown?
Bricks are brown.

Guy Joseph (11)
Coten End Primary School, Warwick

The Hill

Mist covers the hill
Covers it like a white blanket
The hill is asleep
It will be woken by the morning dew
In the summer children play, too hot for dew
Back in winter on the Scottish hill
All is dead but the hill hangs on
Waves clash against the ragged rock but the hill hangs on.

Lucy Edwards (10)
Coten End Primary School, Warwick

Dream Bedroom

If I could have a bedroom
The bedroom of my dreams
I'd make the carpet sparkle
Just like a flowing stream.

The curtains would be lilac
The wallpaper pink
I'd have a nice cold fridge
For whenever I need a drink.

My bed would be really tall
With a ladder to reach the top
There would be a pink telly up there
And lots of cans of pop.

I'd have a puppy too
To cuddle when I'm sad
He'll behave if I want
If I don't, he'll be bad

I don't mind if I don't
Have my dream bedroom
I get it if I want to change
Which I don't think will be soon.

Georgina Lamb (11)
Coten End Primary School, Warwick

Marshmallows

Soft in my mouth
Gooey and tender
Different colours
White and pink
Sweet like sugar
Sticks to my fingers
Stretchy all over
Spongy and thick.

Martin Brown (11)
Coten End Primary School, Warwick

Midnight Sky

As I look through my window,
I see the midnight sky,
I see the bats ready to fly,
I see the big white moon.

As I go through the deserted park,
I see what I've never seen before,
Bats hanging upon the several trees,
I wade through grass above my knees,
The swings are no longer swinging.

Magical midnight, magical midnight,
I watch it as it fades away.

As I look through my open window,
I see the sun in the sky,
I see the birds ready to fly,
The blazing sun takes its place,
Everyone's wearing sun tops with grace.

As I walk through the fun-filled park,
It is no longer dark,
The grass is no longer above my knees,
Where are the bats from the trees?
Birds take their place.

So I sit here in my window waiting
For the midnight sky.

Abigail Smith-Howells (11)
Coten End Primary School, Warwick

The Sea - Haiku

Sea reflects the sun,
The sand is warm on our feet,
Sun shines everywhere.

Kimberley Williams (10)
Coten End Primary School, Warwick

The Ghost

This is the ghost
That doesn't like to boast
He swoops in the sky
But he does like to lie.

He swooped to the school
And met a fool
He went through the wall
And he grew so tall.

He picked up the books
Then took a look
The bell rang
So the children sang.

He went through a tree
And met a bee
He went to the pub
And joined a club.

He had a drink
And took a wink
He went home
To see the garden gnome.

He ate his lunch
With a big crunch
It went through his skin
As sharp as a pin.

That's the ghost
That we like the most.

Tim Hood (11)
Coten End Primary School, Warwick

Football

They play outside, the ball is the main thing
Always a footy match on days like these
As it gets exciting, the bell will ring
The teacher blows the whistle and they freeze

I love this game, though they say it's for boys
I don't know why I play it, I just do
Tackle, kick, pass the ball and ignore the noise
Could score a great goal if I wanted to

All football matches are nearly the same
After the game you're always out of breath
Play for fun, play to win, it's just a game
Like most of these things where it's life or death.

Danielle Scott (11)
Coten End Primary School, Warwick

The New Head Teacher

The new head teacher
She rules the school
Horrible, strict, huge
She talks like a herd of rhinos
She marches down the corridor like a mass of elephants
It makes me feel scared
Like a mouse getting chased by a cat
The new head teacher
We have to live with it.

Amy-Louise Morgan (11)
Coten End Primary School, Warwick

The Platypus

There was a platypus called Billy
He ate a hot and spicy chilli
The platypus, he went bright red
Collapsed on the floor, was nearly dead

The chilli was going to work on his liver
He got up quickly and rushed to the river
He got himself a loaf of bread
And rocketed back to his watery bed

He went round to his mate next door
But he was lying on the floor
Billy said, when he saw the chilli,
'How could you have been so silly?'

Ben Miller & Joshua Baker (11)
Coten End Primary School, Warwick

My Angel

My angel
Came from Heaven
White, soft and bright
It flies in the night
Like my family watching over me
I feel so soft, small and safe
So every night when I am there in bed
I never worry because I know she's there
My angel
Always looking over me and keeping me out of trouble.

Charlotte Lilley (11)
Coten End Primary School, Warwick

On The Beach

On the beach there is golden sand
Many tourists come and go
The water washes onto the land
Roughly, but in a flow

When it is night, the sky is full of stars
The sea is cold and the moon shines
Nothing can be heard except for the cars
The sea goes in and out on the sand, leaving many wave lines

The sun is creeping into the sky
The water crashes and crushes on the rocks
Seagulls are spreading their wings and start to fly
Ships have come to find the docks

In the town families are preparing for a day at the sea
The lifeguards are patrolling the boats
Children are splashing in the sea
The sun is out, no need for coats.

Edward McEwan (10)
Coten End Primary School, Warwick

Swings

Swings go high
Swings go low
Swings go click clack co

I go high
I go low
I go, 'No, no!' when I go

When I come back
I dress up in black
Then I pretend that I can fly
On the swings up, up so high.

Rebecca Robinson (10)
Coten End Primary School, Warwick

Football

Football is a game
About working as a team to win
There is a wide field
Open to you, but your way
To the goal is blocked
By eleven tough guys
They are neither your enemy
Nor your opponents
They are your competitor
The tougher the competitor the harder the game
Their business is to stop you
And defend their goal
Your aim is to score a goal
Sometimes you get injured
But if you trust your team
They won't give up until it's their victory.

Prashant Roka (11)
Coten End Primary School, Warwick

Dodgems

The bell rings,
Drivers fling,
Horns blare,
Cars as fast as a hare,
Bumpers crash,
Some become trash,
Joe's on top,
Time to stop,
Go again?
Not in Joe's reign!

James Shacklock (11)
Coten End Primary School, Warwick

True Love

I travelled to a distant land
That's in the shape of a giant hand
And there I saw pretty Eleanor
Captured and chained by Prince Seadore
I vowed to save her and make her my wife
And kill Prince Seadore with the blade of a knife.

Two days later I set her free
And Prince Seadore was as dead as can be
I sailed home with my pretty bride
But she did not stay by my side
She ran away with the King of Tor
Oh! Oh! My pretty Eleanor.

Hannah Ingram (11)
Coten End Primary School, Warwick

Mother Nature

Mother Nature is everywhere
She's been around for thousands of years
Animals and plants will never leave us
You're scared to touch small creatures
You think you might kill or hurt them
One thing dies and another thing lives
And just remember this:
Mother Nature is always there
And it shows nothing really ever dies.

Lewis Coulson (10)
Coten End Primary School, Warwick

The Snake

Crawling through the canyon
 creeping up the road
Slithering in the grass
 trailing across the field
Moving past the forest
 along the sandy desert
Slipping across the rapids
 creeping around the ruins
Leaving trails behind in the creek
 advancing down the mountains
Hissing in the crisp air of the bay
 searching in the volcano
Yet no one notices how I move.

Jonathan James (11)
Coten End Primary School, Warwick

My Mum

My mum
She is wonderful
Kind, helpful, tidy
Like an angel in Heaven
Like a sweet nurse
It makes me feel happy
Like my mum has just kissed me
My mum
Just like my mum thinks of everything for me.

Sira Mahmood (11)
Coten End Primary School, Warwick

The Loch Ness Monster

A benighted, blundering image,
Isolated, inscrutable, allegorical.
What lies beneath the unperturbed waters
Is a sombre sight to suffer.

For the conspicuous Loch Ness monster
Hides its grotesque face.
Fish rush away, appalled at such repellent looks
And the demon hangs his head.

But this beast is not malicious,
Nor malevolent, diabolic or destructive.
It teaches us one mighty lesson,
Looks aren't everything.

Faye Herrington (11)
Coten End Primary School, Warwick

The Brown Teddy Bear

The wonderful brown teddy bear
Is cute and cuddly,
Warm, delicate and soft-hearted,
Like a soft cloud laying on my bed,
Like a cushion on my bed,
It makes me feel safe and joyful,
Like an angel in the sky,
The wonderful brown teddy bear,
Reminds me of how safe you feel when
You are cuddling it.

Charlotte Marshall (11)
Coten End Primary School, Warwick

Life And Football

Life is a game of football
Where you win and lose
The field is open
Shoot for goal if you choose.

Sometimes you get injured
But sometimes you survive
It all depends on the choices
That you make when you arrive.

Cameron Ferguson (11)
Coten End Primary School, Warwick

Summer

I can fly up to the tallest towers,
Without falling in the flowers,
Flowers, sheep, birds everywhere,
But there will be more next year.

Everyone comes to play,
Farmers feed the birds and set the hay,
Summer has nearly ended.

Catherine Pitchford (10)
Coten End Primary School, Warwick

The Eagle

Swirling, swooping around, the eagle flies,
Millions of miles above, we stand and watch on land.

As the great eagle plunges to catch its prey,
The wild roaming animals scamper out of its view.

Everybody be warned,
The harmful eagle may even dine upon you!

Ashleigh O'Connor (11)
Coten End Primary School, Warwick

Lonely Life

As the baby comes
As the baby takes her first breath
She starts to cry

She grows into a child,
It is her first day at school,
She is starting to learn.

She is a teenager now,
She has a lot of knowledge,
She begins to earn money.

She is an adult now,
She is earning a lot of money.
Her skin is beginning to wrinkle.

She is elderly now.
She begins to notice now
Death will come soon.

In the darkness
She calls for her servants
But no one comes.

Hannah Gregg (10)
Coten End Primary School, Warwick

Hallowe'en

Tonight the dead come out to play,
Tonight's the night they have their way.
A midnight party, midnight feast,
Rotten skeletons, zombie beasts,
As the full moon rises, werewolves howl,
Barking and growling as they prowl,
As the clock strikes four,
All the dead fall into the floor,
To spend another year alone,
In a hole they all call home.

Hannah Green (11)
Coten End Primary School, Warwick

A Sugary Sweet

A sugary sweet
Is bad for your teeth
It's purple, round and yummy
And is good for your tummy
It's like a ball
It's very small
You better be careful
Because you might get it stuck
So I'm wishing you, good luck!

Amrita Jhaj (11)
Coten End Primary School, Warwick

My Big Brother

My big brother
Thirteen years of age
Annoying, loud, nasty
Like a giant staring down at me
Like a crocodile always ready to snap
Makes me feel angry
He treats me like a slave
My big brother
Always reminds me that he's boss.

Katy Lawrence (11)
Coten End Primary School, Warwick

Children

Children are leaves playing in the dazzling sunlight
Leaves that skitter off now and again
Light and fast
Small and delicate
But these leaves will never leave the tree completely bare.

Beth Williams (10)
Coten End Primary School, Warwick

The Lion

The lion,
A vicious predator,
Dangerous, cunning, swift,
Like a mighty warrior attacking its enemies,
Like a wanted killer,
It makes me quiver in my boots,
Like a hunted animal,
The lion,
Reminds me that not only humans kill their food.

Kirsty Baker (11)
Coten End Primary School, Warwick

A Special Person

A special person is meaningful,
A special person is treasureable,
Your feelings suffer when you say goodbye,
Hoping it will never end and never have to cry,
You don't want a picture, you don't want their number,
You want them,
A special person is as special as they can be
And my special person is very special to me.

Lindsey Bolitho (11)
Coten End Primary School, Warwick

Leaves

Leaves are cities connected to trees
Cities with a destroying caterpillar
Small eggs
Mighty birds
And at the end of a leaf a cliff that goes on forever and ever.

Lewis Mowat (11)
Coten End Primary School, Warwick

The Eagle

The eagle soars high above us
Scanning the landscape for food
To feed her starving young
She is desperate now
Suddenly a rabbit jumps out of its burrow
The eagle swoops down to catch the rabbit
She has caught it, she has to get it back to her young
But she is tired from a day of hunting
She is determined to get back to her family
The eagle stops on a ledge to have a rest
Minutes later she is back in the air
Now she has arrived back at her young
There is a mad frenzy to get food
This shows us that no matter how hard something is, you can do it!

James Ward (11)
Coten End Primary School, Warwick

My Great Dad

My great dad
34 years old
Magical, wonderful, cheerful
Like someone who never gives up
Like a person who never leaves me
It makes me feel lucky
Like I will never be left alone
My great dad
Reminds me how lucky I am.

Ricardo Spratt (11)
Coten End Primary School, Warwick

The Tornado

It all began one day
A sunny day
A sweltering day
The great almighty sun high in the sky
Its courageous rays gleaming down upon us
But then the sky turned a deep black
Gathering like a crowd of children
Fussing over one another
All of a sudden a grey, spiral object
Came closer and closer and closer
Until the fear built up
And it was so close
It spread its powerful venom all around us
Destroying and terrorising everything.

Laura Cunningham (11)
Coten End Primary School, Warwick

My Cat

My lovely, soft, sweet cat
Only four years old
She's like a tiger but only sweeter
Her teeth are as sharp as needles
It's nice to see her eyes, they make me feel warm
It makes me calm if I'm stressed
Like I'll never be alone again
I know I won't because they will always be here.

Matthew Bennett (11)
Coten End Primary School, Warwick

When I Was One

When I was one
I loved my mum

When I was two
I lost my shoe

When I was three
I got stung by a bee

When I was four
I broke a door

When I was five
I learnt to dive

When I was six
I had a Twix

When I was seven
I went up to Heaven.

Chloe Morris (7)
Croft Junior School, Nuneaton

When I Was . . .

When I was one,
I didn't know anyone.

When I was two,
I went to the loo.

When I was three,
I sat on my dad's knee.

When I was four,
I opened my drawer.

When I was five,
I learned to dive.

When I was six,
I ate a Twix.

Kelly Lobley (7)
Croft Junior School, Nuneaton

When I Was . . .

When I was one,
The sun shone.

When I was two,
I got messy with glue.

When I was three,
I touched a key.

When I was four,
I went to the seashore.

When I was five,
I could not dive.

When I was six,
I had my first Twix.

When I was seven,
My sister took me to Devon.

When I was eight,
I had my own plate.

When I was nine,
The weather was fine.

Kelsey Collins (7)
Croft Junior School, Nuneaton

The Cat Poem

No wings or fins have I
But I am stripy as a tiger
But as cute as a kitten
And I have exciting adventures.

I am fluffy and cuddly and like to be stroked
I never scratch or bite
I make a friend every day while I play
From morning till night.

I sit on the floor watching my friend
Flutter plant to flower hour after hour
Her colours are lilac, blue and red.

I start to play and chase
In the mud all day
Soon it will be dark and time to go home
I hear my master whistle.

I jump over and see my owner
I run with joy
While I eat my food I am happy
I warm up in my nice cosy bed for sleep
Ready for another day.

Lucy Clarke (10)
Croft Junior School, Nuneaton

When I Was . . .

When I was one,
I met a boy called Don.

When I was two,
I found a nice shoe.

When I was three,
I fell out of a tree.

When I was four,
I opened the door.

When I was five,
I saw my mum drive.

When I was six,
I brought a Twix.

When I was seven,
I thought about Heaven.

When I was eight,
I opened the gate.

When I was nine,
I drank some wine.

When I was ten,
I wrote in pen.

When I was eleven,
My sister was seven.

When I was twelve,
I reached the shelves.

Sarah Timms (8)
Croft Junior School, Nuneaton

When I Was . . .

When I was one,
the sun shone.

When I was two,
I met the crew.

When I was three,
I saw a bee.

When I was four,
I went to the seashore.

When I was five,
I saw a beehive.

When I was six,
I learnt some tricks.

When I was seven,
my dad went to Devon.

When I was eight,
I had a plate.

When I was nine,
I heard a wind chime.

When I was ten,
I saw a hen.

When I was eleven,
I went to Devon.

When I was twelve,
I could reach the high shelves.

Amy Bell (8)
Croft Junior School, Nuneaton

When I Was . . .

When I was one
The sun shone

When I was two
I was a fan of Winnie the Pooh

When I was three
I drank a cup of tea

When I was four
I was such a bore

When I was five
I was on TV, live

When I was six
I played with bricks

When I was seven
I thought I was in Year 11

When I was eight
I was hung out to be bait

When I was nine
I had a £10 fine

When I was ten
I had a felt-tip pen

When I was eleven
I kissed a girl who was seven

When I was twelve
I could reach the top shelves.

Connor Whitmore-Lewis (7)
Croft Junior School, Nuneaton

When I Was . . .

When I was one,
The sun shone.

When I was two,
I went to the zoo.

When I was three,
I drank some tea.

When I was four,
I opened the door.

When I was five,
I saw a beehive.

When I was six,
I ate my first Twix.

When I was seven,
I travelled to Devon.

When I was eight,
I saw my best mate.

When I was nine,
I drank some wine.

When I was ten,
I had a pet hen.

When I was eleven,
I thought about Heaven.

When I was twelve,
I could reach the fifth shelf.

Owen Woodward (8)
Croft Junior School, Nuneaton

When I Was . . .

When I was one,
My mum called me Don.

When I was two,
I could tie my shoe.

When I was three,
I cut my knee.

When I was four,
I walked into a door.

When I was five,
I found a beehive.

When I was six,
I collected sticks.

When I was seven,
I went to Devon.

When I was eight,
I ate a date.

When I was nine,
I tried some wine.

When I was ten,
I had a pet hen.

When I was eleven,
My brother was seven.

When I was twelve,
I found a water valve.

Cody Clarke (7)
Croft Junior School, Nuneaton

When I Was . . .

When I was one,
I had a brother called Don.

When I was two,
I couldn't say who.

When I was three,
I ate my first pea.

When I was four,
I could open a door.

When I was five,
We had a new drive.

When I was six,
I ate my first Twix.

When I was seven,
We travelled to Devon.

When I was eight,
We had a new gate.

When I was nine,
I could tell the time.

When I was ten,
I lived in a den.

When I was eleven,
My brother was seven.

When I was twelve,
I could reach the top shelf.

Chloe Tedds (7)
Croft Junior School, Nuneaton

When I Was . . .

When I was one,
I met a man called John.

When I was two,
I learnt how to buckle my shoe.

When I was three,
I cut my knee.

When I was four,
My dad nearly knocked down the door!

When I was five,
My mum taught me how to do a hand jive.

When I was six,
I started to collect sticks.

When I was seven,
I went to visit my auntie in Devon.

When I was eight,
I went on my very first date.

When I was nine,
My brother started to work down a mine.

When I was ten,
My dad caught a hen.

When I was eleven,
My grandad died and went to Heaven.

When I was twelve,
I didn't believe in elves.

Laura Harrison (8)
Croft Junior School, Nuneaton

When I Was . . .

When I was one,
I drew a silly swan.

When I was two,
I was able to buckle my shoe.

When I was three,
I lost my mum's key.

When I was four,
I knocked down a door.

When I was five,
I found a beehive.

When I was six,
I had a cookie mix.

When I was seven,
I flew to Heaven.

When I was eight,
I climbed a big gate.

When I was nine,
I saw somebody's spine.

When I was ten,
I had a hen.

When I was eleven,
I kissed a girl who was seven.

When I was twelve,
I could reach the top shelf.

Nathan Aston (8)
Croft Junior School, Nuneaton

When I Was . . .

When I was one,
My mum had a boy called John.

When I was two,
I learned to go to the loo.

When I was three,
I spotted a big tree.

When I was four,
I fell on a slippery floor.

When I was five,
I wanted to dive.

When I was six,
I cut my lips.

When I was seven,
I knew Jeven.

When I was eight,
I had a date.

When I was nine,
I drank wine.

When I was ten,
I had a hen.

When I was eleven,
I went to Devon.

When I was twelve,
I found a water valve.

Megan Farmer (8)
Croft Junior School, Nuneaton

When I Was . . .

When I was one,
I ate a scone.

When I was two,
I could say 'flu'.

When I was three,
I saw a flea.

When I was four,
I kicked down the door.

When I was five,
I started to dive.

When I was six,
I ate my first Twix.

When I was seven,
My dad went to Devon.

When I was eight,
I met someone called Kate.

When I was nine,
I drank some wine.

When I was ten,
I worked for some men.

When I was eleven,
I wanted to see Heaven.

When I was twelve,
I turned round a valve.

Jake Cleghorn (8)
Croft Junior School, Nuneaton

When I Was . . .

When I was one,
I fed my first swan.

When I was two,
My favourite colour was blue.

When I was three,
I fell down a tree.

When I was four,
I broke down the door.

When I was five,
I learnt to drive.

When I was six,
I liked playing with sticks.

When I was seven,
I met a boy called Jevan.

When I was eight,
I broke the garden gate.

When I was nine,
I drank a bottle of wine.

When I was ten,
I had a pet hen.

When I was eleven,
I got lost in Devon.

When I was twelve,
I could reach the shelves.

Keri-Ann Bishop (8)
Croft Junior School, Nuneaton

When I Was . . .

When I was one,
I had a friend called John.

When I was two,
I loved Winnie the Pooh.

When I was three,
My dad was a referee.

When I was four,
I wanted more.

When I was five,
I could not drive.

When I was six,
I saw sticks.

When I was seven,
I thought I was eleven.

When I was eight,
I saw a crate.

When I was nine,
I drank a glass of wine.

When I was ten,
I went to see Big Ben.

When I was eleven,
I had a trip to Devon.

Faye Glover (8)
Croft Junior School, Nuneaton

When I Was . . .

When I was one,
I had a friend called Ron.

When I was two,
I tied my shoe.

When I was three,
I cut my knee.

When I was four,
I knocked on my gran's door.

When I was five,
I learnt to dive.

When I was six,
I ate a Twix.

When I was seven,
I went to Devon.

When I was eight,
I climbed the gate.

Lucy Fitzsimmons (7)
Croft Junior School, Nuneaton

The Great Heaven

The great Heaven
High in the sky above
Cloudy, beautiful, silent
Like a beautiful garden
Like a sunny day
It makes me feel tingly
Like a furry cat
The great Heaven
Reminds me that the good people
Go up to Heaven.

Ty Marshall
Ewyas Harold Primary School, Hereford

The Secret

I have got a secret
That no one else can share
It is very interesting
My secret I can't bear!

I'll tell you if I wish
But maybe I shouldn't dare!
I really like this secret
And I really care!

You want me to tell you
Maybe, I don't care!
I really don't want to
My secret I will not share!

I have got a secret!
That no one else can share
It is very interesting
My secret I won't share!

Jasmine King (11)
Ewyas Harold Primary School, Hereford

Animals In The Dark

Down in the dark where the elephants grow
The river is flowing and sparkling
The kangaroos are jumping, sleeping and eating
Wherever you bother to go.

Down in the dark where the animals play
They're happy and joyful every day
They stamp in the river and lie on the bank
To God is who they really thank.

Down in the dark where the animals sleep
There isn't a sound, not even a peep
Every night they sleep at a height
Away from all those very big fights.

Christopher Talbot (10)
Ewyas Harold Primary School, Hereford

Inside The Elephant's Trunk

Inside the elephant's trunk, the grey wrinkles
Inside the grey wrinkles, the long brown legs
Inside the long brown legs, the elephant's white teeth
Inside the elephant's white teeth, the taste of juicy fruit
Inside the taste of juicy fruit, the wind's cool breeze
Inside the wind's cool breeze, the elephant's curly tail
Inside the elephant's curly tail, the feel of warm water
Inside the feel of warm water, the elephant's wide mouth
Inside the elephant's wide mouth, the floor's grimy dirt
Inside the floor's grimy dirt, the elephant's plodding stamp
Inside the elephant's plodding stamp, the bluebird's relaxing peck
Inside the bluebird's relaxing peck, the insect's wiggling crawl
Inside the insect's wiggling crawl, the elephant's fat back
Inside the elephant's fat back, the sun's yellow heat
Inside the sun's yellow heat, the elephant's trunk!

Sammi-Jo Lowe (9)
Hall Green Junior School, Birmingham

Inside The Shark's Ears

Inside the shark's ears, swimming shoals of fish,
Inside the swimming shoals of fish, the menacing movement,
Inside the menacing movement, the tiny fish crying,
Inside the tiny fish crying, the enjoyment of his crying meal,
Inside the enjoyment of his meal, the human prey scrambling for life,
Inside the scrambling human, the heart pounding before death,
Inside the heart pounding before death, the shark's mouth,
Inside the shark's mouth, the crunching of the leg,
Inside the crunching leg, the shark's ears.

James Fry (9)
Hall Green Junior School, Birmingham

Inside The Horse's Eye

Inside the horse's eye, the cold stone yard,
Inside the cold stone yard, the mellow green field,
Inside the mellow green field, an icy pond,
Inside the icy pond, the horse's long, pink tongue,
Inside the horse's long, pink tongue, the herbivore's wish,
Inside the herbivore's wish, the horse's scarlet, red heart,
Inside the horse's scarlet, red heart, the love of its foal,
Inside the love of its foal, the twitchy foal's shadow,
Inside the twitchy foal's shadow, a dusty movement,
Inside the dusty movement, the horse's braying call,
inside the horse's braying call, the echo of hope,
Inside the echo of hope, the horse's strongest rear,
Inside the horse's strongest rear, the expanded kick,
Inside the expanded kick, the sun's beating rays,
Inside the sun's beating rays, the horse's eye.

Emily Kennedy (9)
Hall Green Junior School, Birmingham

Inside The Hamster's Ears

Inside the hamster's ears, a sweet gentle voice,
Inside the sweet gentle voice, a whistle of hope,
Inside the whistle of hope, a tiny glint of sadness,
Inside the tiny glint of sadness, the sheer joy of life,
Inside the sheer joy of life, warm drops of tears,
Inside the warm drops of tears, the glowing light of love,
Inside the glowing light of love, the ever-living spirit of prayer,
Inside the ever-living spirit of prayer, the promise of care,
Inside the promise of care, the shining emerald of death,
Inside the shining emerald of death, the hamster's ears.

Katie Clarke-Mullen (9)
Hall Green Junior School, Birmingham

Inside The Shark's Eye

Inside the shark's eye, the long pointed teeth,
Inside the long pointed teeth, the death of life,
Inside the death of life, the ghost's scary cry,
Inside the ghost's scary cry, the sharp blade,
Inside the sharp blade, the tail's blade,
Inside the tail's blade, the searching red eyes,
Inside the searching red eyes, the big black mouth,
Inside the big black mouth, the bold head,
Inside the bold head, the strong bones,
Inside the strong bones, the mighty jaws,
Inside the mighty jaws, the dirty blood,
Inside the dirty blood, the wet grey skin,
Inside the wet grey skin, the power lights,
Inside the power lights, the shark's eye.

Damini Dave (9)
Hall Green Junior School, Birmingham

Inside The Cheetah's Spots

Inside the cheetah's dark spots, the silent whooshing water,
Inside the silent whooshing water, the deer's tear,
Inside the deer's tear, the cheetah's jaw,
Inside the cheetah's jaw, remains of blood,
Inside the remains of blood, the spookiest eyes,
Inside the spookiest eyes, an animal sprinting,
Inside an animal sprinting, a tremble of fear,
Inside a tremble of fear, the cheetah's sharp claws,
Inside the cheetah's sharp claws, the last meal's skin,
Inside the last meal's skin, the cheetah's hurting paw,
Inside the cheetah's hurting paw, the cheetah's spots.

Alison Colgan (8)
Hall Green Junior School, Birmingham

Inside The Scary Lion's Eye

Inside the scary lion's eye, the rustle of the swaying trees,
Inside the rustle of the swaying trees, the lion's fearsome paws,
Inside the lion's fearsome paws, the silence of the soothing jungle,
Inside the silence of the soothing jungle, the lion's frightening jaws,
Inside the lion's frightening jaws, the fabulous, flexible flesh,
Inside the fabulous, flexible flesh, the spirit of life,
Inside the spirit of life, the lion's magical powers,
Inside the lion's magical powers, the lion's bushy mane,
Inside the lion's bushy mane, the tickle upon his face,
Inside the tickle upon his face, the roaring cheerful giggle,
Inside the roaring cheerful giggle, the lion's movement,
Inside the lion's movement, the lion's small ears,
Inside the lion's small ears, the rat's squealing cry,
Inside the rat's squealing cry, the moon's vision,
Inside the moon's vision, the scary lion's eye.

Sannah Mehmood (8)
Hall Green Junior School, Birmingham

Inside The Shark's Ears

Inside the shark's ears, the taste of blood,
Inside the taste of blood, the call of death,
Inside the call of death, the jaws of terror,
Inside the jaws of terror, the fin of shock,
Inside the fin of shock, the human flesh,
Inside the human flesh, the flapping tail,
Inside the flapping tail, the mouth of meat,
Inside the mouth of meat, the big red eyes,
Inside the big red eyes, the rough skin,
Inside the rough skin, the shark's ears.

Kurt Morris (9)
Hall Green Junior School, Birmingham

Inside The Lion's Bushy Mane

Inside the lion's bushy mane, the cub's squeaky cry,
Inside the cub's squeaky cry, meat's hard bone,
Inside meat's hard bone, the lion's fluffy tail,
Inside the lion's fluffy tail, the carnivore's meaty wish,
Inside the carnivore's meaty wish, the lion's sharp fangs,
Inside the lion's sharp fangs, the prey's juicy blood,
Inside the prey's juicy blood, the ground's dirty soil,
Inside the ground's dirty soil, the prey's leg bone,
Inside the prey's leg bone, the licking of tender lips,
Inside the licking of tender lips, the roar of anger,
Inside the roar of anger, the lion's bushy mane.

Zoe Tibbetts (8)
Hall Green Junior School, Birmingham

Inside The Lion's Skin

Inside the lion's skin, its own shiny red blood,
Inside the shiny red blood, the medium sized heart,
Inside the medium sized heart, the animal's skeleton,
Inside the animal's skeleton, the flexible legs,
Inside the flexible legs, the rat's silent cry,
Inside the rat's silent cry, the death forever,
Inside the death forever, the shiny white fangs,
Inside the shiny white fangs, its dark pink throat,
Inside the dark pink throat, its wet red nose,
Inside its wet red nose, the lion's big wide mouth,
Inside the lion's big wide mouth, the lion's skin.

Faisal Qureshi (9)
Hall Green Junior School, Birmingham

Inside The Bat's Ears . . .

Inside the bat's ears, the sound of prey,
Inside the sound of prey, tears crying,
Inside the tears crying, the appearance of jaws,
Inside the appearance of jaws, the dripping blood,
Inside the dripping blood, two sharp, fierce teeth,
Inside the two sharp, dripping teeth, hairy, flapping, black wings,
Inside the hairy, flapping, black wings, the blind eyes,
Inside the blind eyes, the black body,
Inside the black body, the bat's sharp ears,
Inside the *bat's* ears!

Arjun Modhwadia (8)
Hall Green Junior School, Birmingham

Magic Memory

When Nick came I was his friend,
Then the friendship began to bond,
He began to feel comfortable here,
We played on the bars all the time,
Then Aaron came along and joined the gang,
We went on the bus all day and played away.

Then Louis joined the cool club gang,
Every day play away, it's fun, fun, fun,
All we learn are tricks and style,
Playing and acting all the while,
All of us are very good friends,
Laughing and joking in our imaginary world,
The friends we will be, in our family tree.

Daniel De Rosa (10)
Haselor School, Alcester

Magic Memory

The journey was long,
I was bursting with joy.
We were finally there
And there was our baby boy.

My brown speckled pup,
Tiny and small,
He had rolls of fat,
Curled up in a ball.

His coat was silky satin,
Sid was his name.
Ringlets on his floppy ears,
Playing was his game.

On the way back,
I held his fluffy paw.
If I stopped,
He cried for more.

He loved his food,
He was a bit of a pig.
The flowers were up,
As he loved to dig.

He wanted something of ours,
As he didn't want to be apart.
He kept it close to himself,
Like I kept him close to my heart.

Emily Harrison (10)
Haselor School, Alcester

Magic Memory

Walking down a field one day,
With my best friend on holiday,
We saw a blind one-eyed bunny,
He could not see where he was running,
We kept on following until he stopped,
Me and Olli prayed and prayed
And then he started running happily again.

Sebastian Young (11)
Haselor School, Alcester

When I Was Four

I was only four years old
But I knew I should do as I was told
I sneaked in the kitchen at seven
The drink was from Heaven
It fell on the floor
Sprayed the window and door
And that was the end of me.

Nicola Boots (11)
Haselor School, Alcester

Magic Memory

When I got a bike
I couldn't believe my eyes
It was blue and black
When I got dressed
I went out on it
It was very good
I will treasure it all my life.

Jordan Clarke (10)
Haselor School, Alcester

I Will Remember

I will always remember my guinea pig's face,
Her sweet eyes that seem to glow like the sun,
Her nose that greedily sniffs the air for food
And especially her slit mouth open often to squeak for food.

I will always remember my guinea pig's body,
Her podgy stomach that sticks out too much,
Her beautiful fur that gleams like the moon
And how she stretches on a hot day.

I will remember my guinea pig's movement,
The way she scuttles across to her hutch,
How she slouches in her hutch
And especially how she jumps excitedly.

Helen Geddy (11)
Haselor School, Alcester

Magic Memory

I went on my first scout camp,
The tent was very wet and damp,
The woods were very cold and dark,
We always lit a campfire,
But that still didn't warm us up,
We went to play games on the side,
But the lads just wanted to give it up.

Louis Randall (11)
Haselor School, Alcester

Magic Memory

My magic memory was when my dog was six weeks old
Me, Mum, Dad and Jack went to see him
He was warm, small, cute and cuddly
It was the best day of my life.

Lewis Seabright (11)
Haselor School, Alcester

Magic Memory

G etting ready for my exam
R ushing and raging
A round the house
D esperate to know what would happen
E veryone ready to take me

O ver and over I practised
N ever thought I'd pass
E veryone cheered when they heard.

Emily Bennett (10)
Haselor School, Alcester

Magic Memory

I was puzzled
When I saw my old house bare
Upset to say goodbye to many friends
I was tired from looking round houses
Bored as well from travelling
Excited to make new friends
And enjoy the new house
Glad when I saw all my toys unpacked.

Ben Jackson (10)
Haselor School, Alcester

Cricket

The first time I ever held a bat
The first time I played cricket
The first time I played for a club
Thanks Trevor
For teaching me cricket.

Nicholas Gardener (10)
Haselor School, Alcester

My Magic Memory

My first day of school
I had no friends anywhere
I sat down at a desk
Opposite an empty chair

A girl came along
And sat down at the seat
Her name was Lauren Statham
Her strawberry hair so neat

At first I thought she's weird
But then I understood
She was the one
The one that could . . .
Be my best friend forever!

Jessica Rice (11)
Haselor School, Alcester

Magic Memory

I remember my aunt was going to have a baby
Will it be a girl? Maybe!
I felt the baby kick in my aunt's tummy
When I let go I felt all funny
Went into hospital on a snowy day
I was glad I had gone all that way
There was a baby wrapped in pink
She was so beautiful I couldn't think
I put my finger on her soft toe
She grabbed my finger and wouldn't let go
Megan is what we called her
When she was born she had hair like fur.

Phoebe Parkes (9)
Haselor School, Alcester

Magic Memory

A magic memory to me
Is something very special,
That I'll think about forever
And this I'll share with you.

I've got a lot of good memories,
That I would like to share,
But this one is the best
And will stand out everywhere.

I had to go to hospital
And have an operation,
I woke up afterwards
To find Mum's hand on mine.

That's when I knew,
She was special to me
And that's why she's perfect,
For my magic memory.

Joshua Kitchen (11)
Haselor School, Alcester

Magic Memory

My magic memory is special to me
So come and listen and I will tell you all about it

There was a new boy called Lawrence
He was a really good friend to me
We played together forever and ever
And never fell out with each other

When I first came to this school
I didn't know what to do
But two boys called Lewis and Josh showed me around
And they are really good friends.

Luke Nicholson (10)
Haselor School, Alcester

My Magic Memory

My magic memory
Is most marvellous of all
Because I've known my dad and mum since I was small
And still remember them at 11 years old

This is special to me
Because without my magic memory
I wouldn't remember my parents
Being there for me

My parents are precious to me
Because without them
There would be no one to encourage me.

Gabby Cook (11)
Haselor School, Alcester

I'm Hungry

I want a bowl of ice cream
I want a plate of chips
I really want a tasty feast that'll
Make me lick my lips.

I'll have a bar of chocolate
I'll have a slice of cake
Any food that I can see
I will quickly take.

Now I'll eat up all the ice cream
I'll eat up all the chips
I'll eat up all the chocolate and cake
Which I simply had to take.

Yummy, yummy, yummy
Oh no! Bellyache!

Scott Corbett (10)
Hillmorton Primary School, Rugby

Pen

A
Pen
Can
Draw
A
Line
Softly
And
Smoothly
It's
Easy
To
Hold
Ink
Is
Rolling
Down
My
Page
And
This
Pen
Is
Mine.

Adam Stevens (10)
Hillmorton Primary School, Rugby

Elisabeth

Sunday, Monday, Tuesday, Wednesday, Thursday
Five days of screaming, she's got a stinky nappy
She has the hiccups all the time
She cries when she's hungry and burps when she's ill
She lives in my house and sleeps in a cot
She's not having my bedroom!
This is my new niece.

Jason Fulthorpe (8)
Hillmorton Primary School, Rugby

The Funny Iguana

There was an iguana
That had a father,
That lived on the isles
Of Billybongana!

Then the iguana,
That had a father,
That lived on the isles
Of Billybongana,
Went on holiday
And ate a banana.

Then the iguana,
That had a father,
That lived on the isles
Of Billybongana,
That went on holiday
And ate a banana,
Came face to face,
With a naughty llama.

At last the iguana,
That had a father,
That lived on the isles
Of Billybongana,
Ran far, far away from the naughty llama
And now he's being chased by a herd of bananas!

Jack Stewardson (10)
Hillmorton Primary School, Rugby

The Red-Hot Dragon

The red-hot dragon
His tail on fire
His mouth covered in ash
He lives in a cave.

Whoever comes near the dragon's lair
He sprays enormous flames
Out of his mouth
His victim is dead.

When it's lunchtime
He spreads his big, outstretched wings
And flies to find humans to eat.

His name is Komodo
He has claws like blades
And eyes lit with fire
The red-hot dragon is the most
Dangerous dragon of them all.

Scott Webb (11)
Hillmorton Primary School, Rugby

Time

Stare,
Time blows by,
Thoughts repeated,
Never more,
Never less,
Hope rides on starry skies,
Humbly drying song,
Heart beats,
Time stands still.

Lauren Kennedy (10)
Hillmorton Primary School, Rugby

The Elephant's Cry

Elephant nibbling the green grass plain
We arrive and pierce your skin
    We use it for our shoes

You cry for your family
You cry for your kind
We arrive and pierce your skin
    We use it for our coats

We sadden your family
We sadden your kind
We arrive to fetch your tusks
    We use them for ornaments

Instead of leaving you to live
We choose coats and ornaments
These you need but not us
For you need life just like us.

Naomi Scarsbrook (10)
Hillmorton Primary School, Rugby

Outside

The way the breeze
Moves the trees,
Feel the air,
It moves your hair,
The sun is like a lava, hot,
The winter is cool febreze
You can see it in the trees
If you stand outside you'll see
How nice the world can be.

Amy Kennedy (10)
Hillmorton Primary School, Rugby

My Imaginary World

I am startled, all I can see is a big rainbow,
The end seems really low,
Maybe there's gold ahead
That's what the tale said,
I just can't stay still,
I keep running until
A dragon staring with beady eyes,
Well I am quite wise,
This is my imaginary world.

Then I look up above
And I see unicorns flying like a dove,
The dragon flies in the sky,
Then something caught my eye,
Then I realised it was a fairy,
With a colourful canary,
A lot of people have imaginary worlds,
I think some of those people - like me,
Wish that their imaginary worlds would become reality.

Susan Billingham (10)
Hillmorton Primary School, Rugby

Emigration

Blurred pictures
Entering my mind
I talk to her often
But not in the same way
Other side of the world
Night is day
Day is night.

Charlotte Butcher (10)
Hillmorton Primary School, Rugby

The Big Match

Football's good, football's great
With lots of fans
And a referee
So that's football to me.

Kicking the ball is the basic thing
To win the whole game
The goalkeeper will try to stop you
So always watch your back.

Thomas Millett (9)
Hillmorton Primary School, Rugby

My Grandad

He had a cough that was catching
For sure we were matching
His voice was loud and could wake a crowd
He lived far away but came to stay
Then one day illness struck
Like a bad case of luck
Until the day when Grandad was gone
Never to visit again.

Tommie Harris (11)
Hillmorton Primary School, Rugby

My Dad

He is a bouncy sofa
He is a cute and cuddly cat
He is a happy blue tit that sings a lot
He is a rich red poppy in the sun
Growing nicer and nicer every single day
He is a fizzy drink of pop wanting to be drunk.

Samantha Clarke (10)
Hillmorton Primary School, Rugby

Nan

She was straining to be with him,
Then the time came,
She was going up there,
The gates down there were closed,
She finally found him.

Now after six years apart,
They've finally met,
Living happily now,
Looking down from the skies.

I wasn't happy at first,
But I realised,
My nan and grandad,
Happy at long last.

Tommy Hall (11)
Hillmorton Primary School, Rugby

The Dell

I perch on the damp green carpet
To smell the aroma of flowers
The evergreen trees talk in whispers
As a gush of wind hits my face
I gaze at the fluffy cotton wool in
The deep blue ocean up above
I hear the birds singing with joy
Playing around from tree to tree
Passing the shining bulb in the sky
The razor of sun shines on me
Making me feel like a desert creature.

Katherine Cooney (10)
Hillmorton Primary School, Rugby

Hair

Some hair spiky
Some hair long
Short hair likely
Some follow along

Some people have afros
Some people are bald
Some hair goes to and fro
Some hair is old

Some hair weird
Some hair cool
Some big heads
Some look fools.

Russell Pinks (11)
Hillmorton Primary School, Rugby

The FA Cup Final

Fans stomping going to seats,
Next player's out, centre's taken,
Footballers down the pitch,
Shot,
Goalkeeper saves, fans cheering,
Next, foul,
Referee comes over screaming,
Red card is shown,
Penalty taken and . . .
Wow! What a goal,
End of game.

Liam Moore (9)
Hillmorton Primary School, Rugby

The Stars

The stars twinkle in the night
They twinkle very bright
The stars fall from the sky
It makes you tell a wish or admit a lie
The stars are always there
They make pictures and give us a scare
The stars shine and make us stare
They float in the sky with good care
The stars will always be there.

Reece Tranter (10)
Hillmorton Primary School, Rugby

My Grandad

My grandad is like a crumpled up piece of paper
An unfinished puzzle
That will never be finished
He is slowly rotting away
Just like an apple
He is like rain trickling down the road
Slowly, slowly, gone
Never to return.

Olivia Abbott (11)
Hillmorton Primary School, Rugby

Here Is A Field

Here is a field where dandelions grow
And breezes blow

Here is a field where I may lie
And stare at the sky

Here is a field where rabbits hop
Out of their burrows and into the sun.

Jamie Newman (10)
Hillmorton Primary School, Rugby

God

When God is sad and crying
The sky turns black
And the sky makes thunder
And lightning comes and destroys
Everything in its path

When God is happy
The sky is clear and nice and sunny
We all play in the sun at morning and evening
And all the children have a fun time

When God is running
The ground shakes
And makes earthquakes and landslides
It makes things fall apart.

William Ratcliffe (10)
Hillmorton Primary School, Rugby

Pets

There once was a hungry cat
Who ate a delicious rat
The bones got stuck
Brought him bad luck
That was the end of that

There once was a huge dog
Who swallowed a tiny frog
He bit a stick
Had a good lick
Then sat on a log
In the fog.

Willow Harris (9)
Hillmorton Primary School, Rugby

My Family

My mum and dad, two brothers and me
We fight like Trojans
And sing with glee

When my dad gets angry, he really does shout
And we go to our bedroom
And let him chill out

My mum is like a bomb
Ticking away until we do something wrong
Then it is an explosion

My family is just like any other
We all love each other.

Alex Walker (11)
Hillmorton Primary School, Rugby

Beach, Beach, Beach

Rock stands on sand
Sand gets wet seas
Sea cramped with fish
Fish swim on the seabed
Seabed covered in seaweed
Seaweed washes on the beach
Beach covered in litter
Littler under deckchair
Deckchair on poem
Poem is over
Over this poem is.

Emily Mann (8)
Hillmorton Primary School, Rugby

Darkness On The Town Of Macensgrove

As the darkness creeps up on the town of Macensgrove,
As the light is pushed into an invisible alcove,
The tomcats slither out from their daily refuge
And pounce about the night, as like a scrooge
The people of Macensgrove flee from the scene
As the darkness shadows the town, at first unseen
The citizens are swarming locusts, retreating to their homes,
Retreating from their blackened town,
They are getting tired now, they change into a nightgown,
But for now, the tomcats rule the night,
But sink away when it is light,
Yes dawn is now near, the light takes a peep,
As the people are waking,
The town comes alive, the tomcats prowl away,
Because once again, it is day.

Sarah Parsons (11)
Hillmorton Primary School, Rugby

My Dog

My dog's a silly dog,
He's a chasing, racing, crazy dog,
My dog's a happy, funny puppy,
A loving, lick your hand dog,
My dog is my dog.

He's full of grins and smiles,
For he chases his tail,
All around the floor,
I just love my doggy.

Madalaine Vale (9)
Hillmorton Primary School, Rugby

My Best Friend's Gone

Cancer, blindness, deafness,
Slowly kills my best friend,
Rotting him inside, eating him alive,
Making him suffer.
Anorexia hits him too,
He was skin and bone when it got through,
Going away from me, being taken away,
As I had my last cuddle with him, he shook with fear,
He didn't know where he was, he was blind,
As I said goodbye before I left for school,
I came home to see my precious baby puppy was gone!

Sophie Jones (11)
Hillmorton Primary School, Rugby

My Little Sister

My little sister is such a spoilt brat,
She wants, she gets
That's how it stays.

She wants any toys she likes
She gets them just like that
She likes everything
But she likes shinies the most.

Sarah Collier (11)
Hillmorton Primary School, Rugby

My Mum

If I cry and have a bug
You're the one to give a hug

If I die and go somewhere far
I would write your name on every star

That's my mum!

Emma Staley (10)
Hillmorton Primary School, Rugby

Life

Life is just a big adventure that just keeps on going on
As the trees and flowers grow
Everyone just keeps on going on
As the sun rises in the morning
And then sets in the evening
Nobody stops to take a breath

As people go to that better place up in the sky
We're still down here praying for them to come back down
As they just float away in their new good life up in the sky
We all just wish that for one day we cold go and join them
But we cannot, so we just can visit them in our heads
The old nice thought of playing with them back all over again.

Adam Fletcher (11)
Hillmorton Primary School, Rugby

The Weeping Climber

She was sitting in the back with me,
Tears flowing slowly down my cheeks,
They came, she went,
She was gone.
That was the last I saw of her,
I missed her but she slowly trickled from my mind,
My troubles came as she went,
She was a jewel on a ledge,
I was a climber who couldn't reach her,
The jewel fell down into the river,
I waited, I am waiting, for her to come up
Or me to go down myself.

Lauren Rowlands (11)
Hillmorton Primary School, Rugby

Space

I stare up from my room
Looking at space
Looking at Jupiter with its big red spot
Then I look at Mars which is just a dot
We all look at Venus which we haven't seen since the 1200s
Then there is Saturn
Which has a pretty pattern
Then I look at Mercury which is very, very curvy
Then there is Uranus
Which catches all of us
There's something in the sky
That really caught my eye
It was the moon all bright and white
Which is in the sky all very light.

Georgia May (10)
Hillmorton Primary School, Rugby

Days

Mondays are boring
Mondays are bad

Tuesdays are good
But sometimes sad

Wednesdays are a rush
And always mad

Thursdays are great
As there's one day left

Fridays are cool as
There's no more school!

Emma Brown (11)
Hillmorton Primary School, Rugby

The Big Match

Fans stomping
Going to seats
Friends meeting
Feeling the heat
Players out
Centre taken
Players attacking
Defending and fouling
Whistle blows
Red card shown
Penalty taken and . . .
Wow! A goal!
Finally half-time
Players out
Ready to go
Centre taken
Had a long run
And . . . what a goal!
Final whistle gone
We won!

Curtis Jones (8)
Hillmorton Primary School, Rugby

Life

Life is like a piece of dirty gum stuck to the floor
A spot of rain on a sunny day
Disliked, hated and people wishing you were dead
Life is like a broken heart
Like being shot in a battle
Or being trodden on by a giant
Life is like a piece of gum.

Thomas Mitchell (11)
Hillmorton Primary School, Rugby

Jack!

Why have one?
Why do I need one?
Annoying
Teases me
Jumps on my bed
Has *five* girlfriends!
Doesn't let me play with him
Pushes me over
Rips all of my pictures up
Snores in bed too loud, just to annoy me
I can never watch telly because
He plays on the PlayStation all the time
When we are on the beach
He squirts me with his water pistol
When he comes to my birthday party
He pops all the balloons!
I am glad when he goes to Grandad and Grandma's house!
Older brothers!
Why?

Alice Stewardson (8)
Hillmorton Primary School, Rugby

Jake Thomas

Jake is a very funny boy
He has a lot of fans
I am one of them
He's got a funky hairstyle
And wears cool clothes
I get news off the Internet
And I email him on the computer.

Harry Davies (8)
Hillmorton Primary School, Rugby

Strange, Funny Sort Of Aliens

People sometimes are odd
Like you just plod
The 'my parents are aliens' idea
Makes me laugh and sneer.

Sometimes aliens can turn into things
I would just go and hide behind a bird's wings
But they are unnatural, unusual and freaky
But I want to be cheeky.

Aliens have horrible adhesive goo
It is over the top of the loo.

But aliens are mysterious
And I don't know what they eat
But I see it on a seat.

I don't know if they know about holidays
They will be confused
Because they won't know what it says.

Tracey Beaker is so difficult and solid
And I am delighted because she is fabulous
She can knock down the aliens dead
She can make them into bread.

Danielle Bryn (9)
Hillmorton Primary School, Rugby

Robin Hood

A bow like the wind
The silvery gold
Of the point
Ready to be fired
On his prey
Like a deer
A very sparkly point.

Jamie Upton (9)
Hillmorton Primary School, Rugby

God

God has powers
He uses them from above the clouds
He is like thunder
He wanders around
God is lightning above His height
God is amazing
He is not lazing around
He uses His dog for pounding
God is blunt
He will want to hunt
He gives you hope
And He gives you love
God will give you life
You go to Heaven when you die
God will help you if you're stuck
If you are on a hook
God will guide you all around
He will not hound at you
He won't give you a new dad
The first one you had
If it rains, it's a real pain
If it thunders, it will thunder
If it shines, we will pine
God will love you, but who?

Jasmine Urry (10)
Hillmorton Primary School, Rugby

The FA Cup Final

People that play football
People running down the line
So funny when they slide tackle the player
It is so funny
It is a goal by Shane,
End of game.

Shane Osborne (8)
Hillmorton Primary School, Rugby

Sh, Sh, Sh

When you're walking down an alley
And you suddenly see David Beckham,
With Romeo and Brooklyn,
Would you scream?
Would you screech?
Or would you suck all your breath in?

Here I am laying on my bed,
Looking through my bedroom window,
No wildlife about,
No children to shout,
Just me breathing with my dreams!

Laura Manning (8)
Hillmorton Primary School, Rugby

The Cake

It's my brother's birthday
He's turning ten
Although he's not very funny then
My mum is baking his cake
It is his special birthday cake
He likes the computer
He likes kangaroos
They bounce around like little roos
I'm wrapping his present
Of a toy kangaroo
Although he's got so many
He loves kangaroos.

Jessica Scarsbrook (8)
Hillmorton Primary School, Rugby

Roller Skates

I'm nearly down
With a frown
I'm going slowly
I'm going fast
Oh no! I'm down with a crash
I get up off my butt
I'm going again
Look! I'm bleeding
It's coming down fast
I'd better get home quick
Or I might be sick
With all the blood pouring out
The next day
We went to the bay
With my friends
Then we went to play on our roller skates
I am so fast
I'm the best in my class

So here I am 10 years later
I'm here! I'm here at the championships!
I'm race number 10
It's race number 9
I'm next, I'm next!
I'm on the floor
I'm about to go
I'm going! I'm going!
I'm nearly down
But not with a frown
I'm not down
I'm up
I'm winning!

At last! I'm the winner
I go to the stand
I say a few words

And I demand
That if you can't do it
Just try, try, try
When I was little
I was always falling
But now look at me
I'm the best roller skater
In the world
I've got the gold
I'm the best but I wouldn't have done it
If it wasn't for my roller skates.

Nadine Halcrow (11)
Hillmorton Primary School, Rugby

The Leisure Centre

Ping-pong balls whizzing about
Football where we jump and shout
Swimming where we splash away
Running we do every day
In tennis we hit a ball
Throwing, that we do at school
Exercise that keeps you fit
We enjoy this every bit.

Rebecca Urosevic (8)
Hillmorton Primary School, Rugby

Nothing

In cricket nothing is 'duck'
In tennis nothing is 'love'
In football nothing is 'nil'
But with me nothing is sitting down
Pretending I am ill.

Liam Reynolds (9)
Hillmorton Primary School, Rugby

Springtime

Springtime is a time of happiness.
Things start to grow, like rabbits,
Trees and animals,
We get to go outside
And have some fun
All day long.
We get to do our work outside
And play on the grass
And get new equipment.
We get to go outside
And have some fun
All day long.

Alixe Wilmshurst (9)
Hillmorton Primary School, Rugby

My Pets

My dog
Chased my cat,
My cat
Chased a rat,
That rat
Went down a hole,
Through a mole hole,
Then he met
Mrs Mole,
Who was digging
A very big hole,
Up, up to the ground,
Then the rat said,
'How do you get out?'
Then Mrs Mole said,
'With a shout, this way
This way out.'

Lucy Redfern (10)
Monyash CE Primary School, Bakewell

The Garden Of Rhyme

Once upon a fairy rhyme
I walked into the garden of time
I could not hear my brother whine
As the garden was so fine
Roses and bluebells all in a line

I feel as though I'm being carried away
Though it is never the end of the day
'It's the best garden,' I would say
That is why I will always stay
I'll stay here until the end of May

I am the only one here
I know because I stand and peer
Out of my window towards the mere
But one day I saw a small girl near
I looked close and saw a tear

She was crying because her father had sent her
To run away forever and ever
I said, 'Come with me'
She said, 'Never'
I said, 'Please, we could live together'
She said, 'Yes, if you tell me the weather'

I have lived here a very long time
Living here in the garden of rhyme
With my new friend, Heather
She is very, very clever
Now we live together in the garden of rhyme.

Michi Burrow (8)
Monyash CE Primary School, Bakewell

The Match That Ended One-All

I was playing on the football pitch
When Dad scored a goal, wahey!
Manchester Utd are one-nil up, wahey!
Liverpool are going up the pitch
They hit the post, oooh!
The first half score is one-nil
To Manchester Utd
The second half began
Liverpool scored one, oh yeah!
So it was one-all
So it ended
One-all.

George Swindell (8)
Monyash CE Primary School, Bakewell

Playtime

The bell will go any second,
2 o'clock, 1, 2, 3, ring, ring, ring,
Playtime,
Come on, let's go,
Football time,
We get kick-off,
Quick, pass to Jack,
He'll get ya, pass to Tom,
No, it went out,
On my head, George,
Yes goal, *woo-hoo!*

Louis Edge (9)
Monyash CE Primary School, Bakewell

The Moonfairy

I am a moonfairy,
A moonfairy am I,
I twinkle in the moonlight
And float like a kite,
My silver-purple coat,
I'm not one to gloat,
But I'm the prettiest fairy around,
My magical wings don't make a sound,
I am the moonfairy,
The moonfairy am I.

Bethany Swindell (10)
Monyash CE Primary School, Bakewell

Lucky Leprechaun

Leprechauns, leprechauns everywhere
You may not see them but they are there
They live in trees with knobbly knees
But they try to stay away from bees

They make you really lucky
But they do tend to be quite mucky
They don't like the rain
You can say that again.

Bryony Swindell (9)
Monyash CE Primary School, Bakewell

Winter

Arctic-explorer
Window-wrecker
Boat-sinker
Dragon-tooth.

Edward Bloomfield (9)
Moor Park School, Ludlow

Blessing For A Rose

May your perfect petals always be ripe-red,
May your perfume smell as sweet as honey,
May your beauty never be dismantled
And your flowers be freshly rained on every day
And until we meet again,
May God hold you in the palm of His hand.

Vita Unwin (8)
Moor Park School, Ludlow

Autumn Acrostic

A pple picking for farmhouse cider
U nbeatable firework displays
T rying on warm clothes
U ltimate fruit fantasy
M ountainous bonfires
N ever wanting to get out of bed.

Bruce Maitland (9)
Moor Park School, Ludlow

Wind

Door-knocker
Tree-swayer
Streamlined-flyer
Ground-trampler.

Charlotte Nott (9)
Moor Park School, Ludlow

The Acorn

I tried in vain
But could not find
The acorn nest I'd left behind

I looked on ground
But could not see
The acorn nest that I'd let flee

I looked on man
I looked on beast
But could not find the squirrel's feast.

Hannah Tomes (9)
Moor Park School, Ludlow

Snow

House-hider
Flower-killer
Bush-burier
Car-coverer
Branch-blanketer.

Danielle Round (9)
Moor Park School, Ludlow

Wind And Ice

Wheel-skidder
Shoe-slider
Slit-searcher
Door-stabber.

Edward Wilson (9)
Moor Park School, Ludlow

Wouldn't It Be Funny?

Wouldn't it be funny if
A tiger went *squeak*
And a mouse when running went *roar*?
Wouldn't it be funny if
We went *pop*
And a cork when pulled went *ouch*?

Wouldn't it be funny if
A cow went *zoom*
And a car while racing went *moo*?
Wouldn't it be funny if
A slug went *stomp*
Whilst a foot when walking went *squelch*?

Wouldn't it be funny if
A tap went *quack*
And a duck when laughing went *drip*?
Wouldn't it be funny if
A clock went *bang*
And a bomb when falling went *tick-tock*?

Wouldn't it be funny if
A bee went *whack*
Whilst a fist when hitting went *buzz*?
Wouldn't it be funny if
A biscuit went *bump*
Whilst we when falling downstairs went *crunch*?

Wouldn't it be funny?
Well, wouldn't it be funny?
Well, wouldn't it be funny like that?

Imogen Harley (9)
Moor Park School, Ludlow

Wind

Hair-blower
Window-smasher
Leaf-hurler.

Jessica Hogan (9)
Moor Park School, Ludlow

Wind

Rhino-breather
Nest-destroyer
Nose-blocker
Roof-exploder.

Jack Jones (9)
Moor Park School, Ludlow

The Stag

The three kings rode to the woods one day,
The banners behind them in royal display,
The thunder of hooves on the forest floor,
Made such a din as was never heard before,
And the dappled light from the lofty trees,
Danced and flickered in the swirling breeze,
They galloped and cantered, the wind in their hair,
Then gasped at the sight that awaited them there.
Drinking from a gurgling stream,
Was a stag, with huge antlers agleam,
With shining skin and sparkling eyes,
Like moons hung high in winter skies.
They stalked the stag on that sunny day,
Like an eagle hunts its prey,
They caught the stag and bound it tight,
That wonderful deer with eyes like the night.
'Now I'll take it to my castle where the west wind blows'
'I'll never see such treasure in lands such as those'
'I want all of this fabulous beast'
'I want the best of the bountiful feast'
On hearing this outburst, fury and rage,
That shook the tall knights and the little young page,
The stag leapt from the ropes that tied it up tight,
It ran from the clearing on silver hooves so light.

William Critchlow (10)
Newcroft Primary School, Shepshed

Cats

Cats bounce
Cats pounce
Cats get in a muddle
And fall in a puddle
Cats purr
When you stroke their soft fur
And when you tickle their tummy
They cry for their mummy
When they sleep
They don't count sheep
Cats eat Kit-e-Kat
Then sleep on a mat
They don't need to catch mice
They are far too nice.

Elizabeth Critchlow (8)
Newcroft Primary School, Shepshed

My Cousins

I have seven
They really make me mad
Though I like their dad
They really make me mad
Lydia and Phoebe are the twins
Ella is the next on the family tree
Liam is the only boy and he's crazy, boy oh boy
Emily is cool, she used to be bad
There's me in the middle
Then Jordan, she's mad about Madonna
Hannah is the eldest out of us all
Some of them are small
And some are quite tall.

Lucie White (9)
Newcroft Primary School, Shepshed

My Dog

I read a book about a Spaniel
Then I bought one and named it Daniel
We went to the shop
Right to the top
I bought him a bone
He took it and ran straight home
He went to his rug
And tug and tug
He fell asleep
And I had a quick peep!

Elizabeth Clarke (9)
Newcroft Primary School, Shepshed

A New Rabbit

I have a new baby rabbit
It's going in a hutch
I've got a little bowl for it
I'll love it very much

Sometimes I hear it whine
When I'm not around
I got it from a friend of mine
I feed it loads of food.

Bethany Bone
Newcroft Primary School, Shepshed

Humpty Dumpty Comes Back!

Humpty Dumpty is a ghost
Slipping on banana skins
Then falling on a slice of toast!

Alex Hopwood (9)
Newcroft Primary School, Shepshed

Football Crazy

Football crazy! Chocolate mad!
Play football with the lads!
When you kick the ball
You're bound to get a fright
Football crazy! You'll do everything right
Kickin' the ball
Kickin' the ball
Oh, oh, oh.

Matthew Dobson
Newcroft Primary School, Shepshed

Sweets

Chocolate and toffee and a white ice cream cone
I ring up my friend and we're chatting on the phone
I ask what I should get and he said
'Remember the day that we first met
We had chocolate chip ice cream with a medium cornet
But we couldn't eat it because guess who did?
My big fat annoying pet!'

Elizabeth Bray (9)
Newcroft Primary School, Shepshed

Sick On The Plane

There was a young boy from Spain,
Who was travel sick on a plane,
He threw up on the floor,
And all over the door,
So he never went on again.

James Bottomley
Newcroft Primary School, Shepshed

My Brick

My dog is called Brick
My dog is dark
He can do tricks
He always barks

My dog eats pies
My dog has got a long tail
He can wear a tie
He always fails

My dog always talks
My dog likes bouncy balls
He always goes for walks
He always looks at walls

My dog is the best pet
My dog always looks at cats
He always goes to the vet
He always gets a pat.

Lucy Billing (9)
Newcroft Primary School, Shepshed

Fireworks

Fireworks in the sky, up so high,
One, two, three, there and there,
There another one and there and there,
Red, yellow, green and blue,
Catherine wheels spinning round and round,
Rockets shooting high in the sky,
I smell a smell like burning fire,
Oh look, there's a bonfire!
Smoke pouring out, it's hot on my face.

Laura Clarke (6)
Newcroft Primary School, Shepshed

My Dog, Bramble

I have a dog, his name is Bramble
When he gets on the couch he likes to scramble

Now that he is fairly old
He likes to think he's rather bold

When we take him for a walk
He looks at us when we talk

My daddy takes him on the van
And feeds him up with lots of ham

He sleeps in his bed and snores all night
And he doesn't wake up until it's light

In his bowl there's a big chunk of meat
Lying there ready to eat

His heart bumps loud when he runs around
When he's asleep, he doesn't make a sound

When he eats, he chews and chews
Until he poos

My sister, Issie, lies in his bed
Snuggled up into his great big head

When he goes for a walk
He eats lots of pork

When we play tug of war
He goes near the door

He's got a big mouth
He eats lots of food
And all day and night
He chews and chews

Even though he is big and fat
He's my best doggy and that's a fact.

Oliver Mills (9)
Newcroft Primary School, Shepshed

Hectic Hamsters

Rosie, Rose, lots of love
White and snowy as a dove
One day in May she came to stay
She likes to wander and to play
Not very gentle she nibbles the bars
But soon finds out she won't go far!
The bars on her cage they rattle and rattle
I'm never gonna win this battle
She is a very loving pet
She's never ever bitten me - yet!
She likes to wander down the hall
Going fast in her exercise ball
At night when I am trying to doze
She creeps from her bed on tippy-toes
And then she makes the loudest noise
Playing with her little toys
Sleep for me it does not come
I have to wait until she's done
Then back she creeps to her little den
Where she settles down and then
Looking so very warm and snug . . .
I wish I could give her a great big hug!
Rosie, Rosie lots of love
White and snowy as a dove.

Kate Bennett
Newcroft Primary School, Shepshed

Spring

S un shining very bright,
P ink blossom on the trees,
R abbits bouncing to and fro,
I wonder what's coming next,
N ice, pretty flowers swaying in the breeze,
G ates open for spring to rise.

Iony Dewsbury-Martin
Newcroft Primary School, Shepshed

My Westie

My dog's a Westie
He's as white as snow
Upon the field
You should see him go

He runs quite fast
With all his might
When he gets home
It's bed for the night

He rises early
To play with his ball
But his favourite hobby
Is to dig in the wall

He's a cheeky chap
With a high-pitched yap
When a stranger's around
He stands his ground

People who call
Say, 'Ahh, he's sweet'
Until he tries
To chew their feet

Our Westie's a pup
And so soft to touch
We all adore him
And love him so much.

Lauren Grant (9)
Newcroft Primary School, Shepshed

Easter

This is Easter Sunday
Into church they go
Walking so demurely
In a little row

With their dainty bonnets
Dresses long and white
Tiny little sandal shoes
Faces sweet and bright

The church is full of flowers
Spring is here at last
Daisies and buttercups
On the altar cast.

Megan Peat
Newcroft Primary School, Shepshed

Hallowe'en

Horrid monsters roaming the streets,
A bunch of scary-looking creeps,
Lanterns glowing in the night,
Luminous bugs will give you a fright,
Odd-looking hags with broomsticks,
Watch out! Lots of people playing tricks,
Evil spirits let loose to haunt,
Eyes that watch and then will taunt,
Never forget - this is Hallowe'en!

Ellie Bennett (10)
Newcroft Primary School, Shepshed

The Pet Shop

Pets, pets everywhere
Over here, over there
One near you, one near me
Pets everywhere I can see
Hogs, frogs and dogs
Cats, bats and rats
A little kitten curled in a ball
What a pity my mum won't let me buy them all!

Alexandra Oram (9)
Newcroft Primary School, Shepshed

Food

I love my food
I have three meals a day
I shall eat when in a mood
I shall eat when I'm happy

Fish and chips
With peas on the side
They make my lips
Tingle inside

Sausage and mash
With gravy all over
I'll eat in a crash
Even if it spills all over

Pie made with chicken in
All wrapped up in a crust
Is absolutely sickenin'
I'd sooner eat some rust.

Rebecca Law
Old Vicarage School, Derby

The Sound Collector

(Based on 'The Sound Collector' by Roger McGough)

A stranger came down my lane
Greasy, groggy and grey
Stuffed every sound into a sack
And took them all away

The crunching of the leaves,
The tapping of the feet
The miaowing of the cat
The dog chomping his meat

The car horns beeping
The ribbit of a frog
The squeaking of little rats
The woofing of a dog

A stranger came this morning
The man came down my lane
He took all the sound away
Life will never be the same.

Joshua Watts (10)
Old Vicarage School, Derby

C.A.T. Spells . . .

Lazy puss
Making fuss
Chasing frogs
Scared of dogs
Mad hissing
Going fishing
My best friend.

Jasmine Rogers (11)
Old Vicarage School, Derby

The Sound Collector

(Based on 'The Sound Collector' by Roger McGough)

A stranger walked through the street,
His clothes were black and grey,
He captured every sound and noise
And carried them away.

The tweeting of the robin,
The woofing of the dog,
The miaowing of the tomcat,
The croaking of the frog.

The roaring of the engine,
The swishing of the wheels,
The rumbling of the thunder,
The little children's squeals.

A stranger walked through the street,
We didn't know his name,
He stole every single sound,
Life will never be the same.

Tom Dring (9)
Old Vicarage School, Derby

The Sound Collector

(Based on 'The Sound Collector' by Roger McGough)

A stranger came up our street,
Looking greasy and grey,
Stuffed every sound into a sack
And dragged them away.

The roaring of the lorry,
The whistling of the bike,
The beep of a super car,
The mumble of the trike.

The barking of a puppy,
The crying, ginger cat,
The squawking of a swallow,
The flapping of a bat.

A stranger came up our street,
He didn't leave his name,
Left us only in silence,
Life will never be the same.

George Sutherland (11)
Old Vicarage School, Derby

Friend Wanted

My friend's got to be
A bit of a laugh
But still have a bath
Not be too bossy
Or else I'll go dotty

My friend's got to have
A good sense in mind
And still be very kind
Sometimes tells lies
But isn't one that cries

My friend's got to like
Going toy shopping
But not really like hopping
Also like football
But not be too tall
That's what my friend's got to be.

Caroline Morris (10)
Old Vicarage School, Derby

Daily Diary

On Saturday I sat and sadly contemplated sitting my SATs
On Sunday Sammy swam in the sunny shimmering sea
On Monday one mighty mount made me mighty proud
On Tuesday I travelled in a ten ton truck to a shop at
                                    Taylor, Thompson shop
On Wednesday I waited while Wilfred waxed Willy's car,
On Thursday Thora Thurbet thought she'd thoroughly
                                    think things through
On Friday Frankie fought his fears and was free again
On Saturday Suzy sat in the shoe shop and shone and shined all day
On Sunday silly Sally went to see a shocking show.

William Barr (11)
Old Vicarage School, Derby

The Sound Collector

(Based on 'The Sound Collector' by Roger McGough)

A stranger came by today,
Not welcome yet to stay,
Stuffed all the sounds into a box
And dragged them all away.

The squawking of the parrots,
The swishing of the trees,
The roaring of the engines,
The buzzing of the bees.

The bustle of the people,
The honking of a horn,
The rattling of a pushchair,
The yelp caused by a thorn.

A stranger came by today
And played a little game,
Now all we have is silence,
Life will never be the same.

Christopher Houlton (10)
Old Vicarage School, Derby

Wanted - A Friend

I'm looking for a friend and they have to be . . .
Kind and generous, honest, into music, helpful,
Friendly to others, loyal, funny, quite smart,
A girl, slightly mad, fashionable, aged 10 to 10
And three quarters, good looking and not shy!

If you think you are my perfect friend,
Contact me at:
Thatch Cottage
Penny Lane
Blueberry Hill
Scottish Mainland.

Molly Rogers (10)
Old Vicarage School, Derby

A Friend Is A Friend

A friend is a friend,
Religions doesn't matter to me,
Friends tell the truth, sometimes it hurts,
That's why friends are friends.

A friend is a friend,
The colour of your skin doesn't matter,
Friends are there for each other,
That's why friends are friends.

A friend is a friend,
Lame, blind or dumb,
These small things don't matter,
That's why friends are friends.

A friend is a friend,
Short, tall, round or small,
We can see through these differences,
That's why friends are friends.

A friendship is always a friendship,
No matter how big the differences,
Wherever in the world you live,
A friend is a friend.

Kajal Surelia
Old Vicarage School, Derby

My Ideal Friend

I want a friend,
I've been a bit lonely,
I'd love someone,
Who wouldn't own me.

You see, my old friend,
She was mean,
She told me what to do
And said I wasn't keen.

I'd like a humorous girl,
Sporty and daring,
Very pretty and happy,
Clever and sharing.

Friend please find me,
Before it's too late,
I'm sick of my old friend,
I need a new mate!

Sophie Neal (11)
Old Vicarage School, Derby

Recipe For A Friend

Begin with bags full of fun,
Then add some toys and things to do,
With an ounce of intelligence
And a large spoon of kindness
In order for us to get along,
Carefully mix in some support
In case something goes wrong,
Put in playtime and garden fun,
Then cook in the fresh grass
And morning dew for thirty minutes
And serve with giggles!
And in the end you'll have . . .
The perfect friend!

Charlotte Wright (11)
Old Vicarage School, Derby

The Sound Collector

(Based on 'The Sound Collector' by Roger McGough)

A stranger came on our street,
Dressed in black and grey,
He put all the sounds in a box
And carried them away.

The roaring of the engines,
The squeaking of scared rats,
The barking of all the dogs,
The miaowing of some cats.

The clashing of the thunder,
People going on hikes,
The people chomping carrots,
The whizzing of the bikes.

A stranger came on our street,
Looking a bit insane,
The street has gone all quiet,
Life will never be the same.

Finn Brassington-Edwards (11)
Old Vicarage School, Derby

The Jungle

In the jungle where the lions sleep
There are lots of things to meet
Snakes and tigers, cheeky monkeys
All of them for you to see
And there are slimy slugs, spooky spiders
All these bugs
In the air big eagles
Down below small hunting birds
Down deep under you will meet crocodiles
And frogs' feet
In the jungle where the lions sleep
There are lots of things to meet.

William Griffin (10)
St Joseph's Catholic School, Malvern

My Dream

The moon is falling,
The little baby is calling,
The angels are dying,
UFOs are flying.

We are coming,
We are coming,
Our heads come peeling,
Our souls are filling.

The sun is falling,
Animals are leaping,
Trees are flaming,
Houses are burning.

We are coming,
We are coming,
Our heads are peeling,
Our souls are filling.

The sound is stalling,
All I can hear is beeping,
I can still hear beeping,
I am sleeping.

Alex Stockwell (11)
St Joseph's Catholic School, Malvern

See-Saw

I sit on this end and you sit on that,
Hold on tight, or fall on your back,
While I go up, you go down,
And while you go up, I go down.

Rosina Pelusi (10)
St Joseph's Catholic School, Malvern

Cold Creepy Cottage

In the cold creepy cottage
As you enter the kitchen in rage
The pan on the oven starts to rattle
Before your plate turns back to cattle

The wines and the spirits escape
Their corks bombard you in a spiralling shape
The alcohol floods out and fills up the room
In shock you feel like a mushroom

Then the cutlery flies out of its drawer
And you've worked out some things for sure
You've definitely lost your hunger
Plus you won't live much longer!

The wine's now sloshing around your head
The oven turns on and now you are . . .
Dead!

Peter Brankin (10)
St Joseph's Catholic School, Malvern

Movement In The Wind

Trees drape around
In the wind, so gentle
Whispering tall
They sway in the gust
And as it hits your face
It's as if you have been hit
With a passionate kiss

Trees move with a human calmness
As if they are a yoga guru
Slowly and careful
When the leaves fall to the ground
Without a single sound
But they creak and they whistle
When the wind is too strong!

Martha Merrell (11)
St Joseph's Catholic School, Malvern

Granny

The granny's house is like Hell!
She waits for the grandson
Like a tiger, ready to pounce
As soon as he rings the bell.

The granny's house smells like dead skin!
As the grandson enters
He falls, the smell is awful
Even worse than the bin.

The granny's house is stomach-turning!
As she eats the food
You see it, churning in her mouth
Grannies are horrid, the grandson was learning.

The granny's house is like Hell!
The grandson leaves
She will wait, till next time
Next time he rings the bell.

Benjamin Gwyther (11)
St Joseph's Catholic School, Malvern

The Sparkler Incident

Here is a tale about a boy named Tommy
And this little boy is quite a dummy,
You see Tommy loves to play with fire,
He says he doesn't but he's just a liar.

One day Tommy, doing what he loves,
Lit a sparkler without wearing gloves!
The sparkler was actually quite bright
And it gave off loads and loads of light.

The sparks suddenly lit up his head,
He was running around but soon he was dead,
So there is the tale of that little blighter,
So remember this, never play with a lighter!

Jason Alfonso (11)
St Joseph's Catholic School, Malvern

Bats Are Very Clever!

Bats are small and sneaky
They can be very creepy
They fly about at the dark of night
They can give you a terrible fright

Bats come in different shapes and sizes
Big, small and just normal
Eeeaak! they say
To show the way
You may think that they don't need to say this
But if they don't, they'll go bump

There are black bats, brown bats and grey bats
I think you can have blue and purple bats
Did you know they can hang upside down?
Very clever in my opinion

So bats are sneaky and creepy
They can give you a terrible fright
They come in different shapes and sizes
And different colours
And the noise they make is *eeeaak!*

Celia Clements (10)
St Joseph's Catholic School, Malvern

Cheeky Chimps!

Cheeky chimps jumping from tree to tree,
Flying around like a buzzing bee.

Mad monkeys messing around,
Jumping, falling on the ground.

Baby baboons eating baby bananas,
Play around with big baby llamas.

Emily Lewis (11)
St Joseph's Catholic School, Malvern

Five More Minutes!

The alarm clock rings, echoing right into my head,
Oh what I would do for some more time in bed!
It's Monday morning - that means school,
Oh double maths; that's so cruel!
Five more minutes Mum - *please!*

I'm so bored and can't stop yawning -
Lessons are done too early in the morning!
Teacher says our work has to be done
Or we'll stay in at break and miss the fun
Five more minutes teacher - *please!*

I'm outside gossiping with my friend,
Sitting in the stuffy classroom drives me round the bend!
The sun is shining and is getting quite hot,
Oh, the bell has rung - that's our lot!
Five more minutes - *please!*

Yes! It's the end of the day,
I've survived the miserable Monday!
I grab my bags and charge to the door,
I don't have any lessons today anymore . . .

Then I remember I have detention!

Jenna Laverick (11)
St Joseph's Catholic School, Malvern

Winter

Snowflakes . . . dancing through the air like fairy's,
Frost . . . freezing all in its wake like a carpet of ice,
Wind . . . whipping your face like the ice-fairy's leash,
All of these traits cage you in,
Winter, like icicles daring to spike you.

Beatrix Hull (10)
St Joseph's Catholic School, Malvern

Bird

If I was a bird,
I would be the luckiest bird,
My wings could touch the softest object in the world,
The clouds.

If I was a bird,
I would be the luckiest bird,
I would sleep in the top of the tree
And dream of the best dream ever.

If I was a bird,
I would be the luckiest bird,
I could swim in the sea
And stand in the desert.

I hope I can be a bird,
The luckiest bird in the world.

Mayumi Lactao (11)
St Joseph's Catholic School, Malvern

The Ocean Whale

Down below the waves of foam,
There's a sound, a bellowing tone,
Hear the noise you're sure to know,
The way it goes it sounds so low.

Below the water bubbles,
The pace of the waves it doubles,
Men in boats must be aware,
They might be in for a real scare.

This mammal is in danger,
So get up from your manger,
Can't you see they need our help,
Do something about it, don't yelp!

Lauren Baddeley (11)
St Joseph's Catholic School, Malvern

Lost At Night!

The night is dark,
The wind is cold,
To give you a chill,
If you are bold.

Misty white clouds,
Blocking the moon,
Is murder quite near?
Blood will drip soon.

The howling wind,
Like werewolves' cries,
It makes me shiver,
A person dies.

Midnight has struck,
No one's around,
Is anyone there,
Where is the sound?

Where's my front door,
I want my home,
I stand here all still,
I am alone.

What can I do?
Where can I go?
My mind needs to think,
I know, I know!

Walk to the light,
Do I live there?
I just cannot tell,
Please someone care!

Laura Burston (11)
St Joseph's Catholic School, Malvern

The Hideous Thing

The hideous thing
It snarls and growls
Its slimy body growling
With bugs and beasts

The hideous thing
Its hair covers it
The hair hides boils
And more vile things

The hideous thing
The feet reeking
Of old rotten red apples
Not to be smelt

The hideous thing
Its teeth are huge
Its green eyes glow red
The nose leaks snot

The hideous thing
This hideous thing
Is *me* before a
Good old soapy bath.

Jonathan Tyrrell (11)
St Joseph's Catholic School, Malvern

Fire

F ire - I am hot, black, burning,
 I am red, orange, hurting,
R ed, no one likes me, I hear beeping,
E nded, it ended, I was put out by my weakness,

Weeping, weeping.

Max Laventine (10)
St Joseph's Catholic School, Malvern

All The Fun Of The Fair

All the fun of the fair
Ride all the rides there
All the fun of the fair
Or win a teddy bear

The helter-skelter is great
Go to the top with your mates
Swivel down, round and round
Until you get all the way down

The big wheel is fun too
It is higher than me or you
In the seat with your friend
Hoping it will never end

The merry-go-round is alright
It definitely won't give you a fright
If you want a gentle ride
Go on the merry-go-round, don't hide

Dodgems are very fast
You'll never be last
Turning round all the way
You could go on dodgems all day

All the fun of the fair
Ride all the rides there
All the fun of the fair
Or win a teddy bear
All the fun of the fair!

Samantha Earnshaw (11)
St Joseph's Catholic School, Malvern

Sweety Treats

Candyfloss is soft and fluffy
Like clouds in the sky
It doesn't make you feel puffy
But I do wonder why

Sherbet is sour and fizzy
Melting in my mouth
Eat too much and I'll go dizzy
It could affect my health

Chewits are so chewy
That's where they get their name
They go all soft and gooey
It's all in the game

But chocolate is my favourite treat
It is so smooth and scrummy
It's something that I like to eat
And feels real good in my tummy.

Mmmm!

Abigail Neal (9)
St Joseph's Catholic School, Malvern

World War II

Many men are falling
They can hear their families calling
Much famine sweeps the land
Every town and place needs to lend a hand

Every family hopes their son will come back
And I bet they want to give Hitler a whack
Bullets shoot everywhere
And Hitler doesn't care

That's war!
Which many saw.

Luke Crocker (11)
St Joseph's Catholic School, Malvern

What Happened When I Tried To Write This Poem?

I tried to write a poem
Of thirty lines long,
I spent a few hours thinking
But nothing came along.
Then after several attempts
It all went very wrong,
I knew I had to think,
Again nothing came,
My mum said, 'Just write lots
Of words down to get your thoughts going.'
All of my words just came out wrong
And I was feeling tired,
I do not think I am a poet
And thirty lines is rather long
I wish I did not have to do it,
I wish I was on another planet.

Francis Grimshaw (10)
St Joseph's Catholic School, Malvern

An Evening Roam

I walked down my dimly-lit street,
the soft pitter-patter of my little feet.

I sighted some cats who were ready to eat,
the corpse of a man whose death came by a beat.

I went into the place with muggers a-plenty
and scary old dogs whose slain was all denty.

I ran the last bit, full of drunken old men,
right into the place that I call my den.

For I am a wolf, hunter of the night
and the two-footed creatures give me quite a fright.

Felix Goodbody (10)
St Joseph's Catholic School, Malvern

My Busy Garden

In my garden where I live,
Is a water fountain
That is colourful,
Red, blue, yellow, orange and green.
The garden has a bench,
The colour is silver, which is very shiny,
With a red stripe.
It is made out of wood.
When it's dark and I'm still outside, the birds sing
A beautiful song.
I also close my eyes and imagine . . .
What it would be like,
To have a *beach garden!*
At the end of the garden there is a rotten shed,
Where all my bikes are kept.
I also have my own den,
My parents call it the child's den.
It has lots of stuff in it.
The garden has a swimming pool, football pitch
And a trampoline . . .
Oh! I mustn't forget the climbing frame.
I love sunbathing by the pool.
My mum has lots of gardening to do,
I would love to help her,
But *I've got to go to school!*
My garden is very busy.

Siobhan Fitzpatrick (10)
St Joseph's Catholic School, Malvern

The Leaf's Journey

The golden leaf fell,
It passed the old well.
It flew around, touched the ground.
It waited.
It waited,
But nothing happened.
Why could it be he fell off the tree?
Why not any other leaf?
A bird flew by, the leaf gave a cry.
He was doomed!
The bird picked him up,
As he got a bit torn.
He was worn,
He was scrunched up,
He looked down with a frown at the other leaves,
He gulped,
The bird stopped.
The leaf looked as he was weaved into the nest,
He tried to look up as some baby birds squeaked.
He looked next to him as a stick spoke,
'You're trapped.'
He gave a sharp poke,
The leaf fell.
He heard a bell,
As a cat lay next to him,
Purr, purr,
The wind blew,
The leaf flew away from the ginger cat.

Anna Cappellina (10)
St Joseph's Catholic School, Malvern

The Beautiful Garden In The City!

In this garden so they say,
It is magical.
With trees that sparkle,
With jewels of great price,
With waters shaped like birds,
And flowers that squirt out of the fountains.

The beautiful garden is pretty,
It is in the city.

In this garden so they say,
It is magical,
It has acres of land
And is awfully grand.

The beautiful garden is pretty,
It is in the city.

Georgia Duncan-Gill (10)
St Joseph's Catholic School, Malvern

The Roman Soldier

Behold the Roman soldier Ney,
He rides through fields of barley and hay,
If he sees a poor farmer there,
He'll kill him then rip out his hair.

Inside he's a nasty man,
He sits at home and eats his devilled ham.
He only fights when he feels like it,
He's a mean little mit (isn't he?).

When he goes off to battle,
He slaughters people just like cattle,
But then an arrow comes along
And hits him in the head, bang on.

Sam Beale (10)
St Joseph's Catholic School, Malvern

Wild Animals

Wild animals running about,
In their languages they shout.

Cheetahs are by far very fast,
In a race they'd never be last.

Horses thud hard around,
You'll remember them, they make a sound.

Bears are extremely big,
They like to dig and dig.

Lions camouflage in the corn,
Waiting for a baby deer to be born.

Tigers with their stripes stand out,
They don't take much hanging about.

Monkeys swing from tree to tree,
They are a wonderful sight to see.

Last but not least, elephants roam free,
That's the way it should be.

Wild animals running about,
In their languages they shout!

Demi Owen (11)
St Joseph's Catholic School, Malvern

Cakes!

C akes are very yummy
A bsolutely scrummy
K ill for a cake
E at the cake
S crummy!

Jazzmyn Robinson (10)
St Joseph's Catholic School, Malvern

Summer

The summer sun
Has just begun
To rise up above the sky
And the birds are coming back to fly

The plants and flowers have opened
And the breeze is warm
With not one storm
And all have joy

The summer is here
Now it's time to go
The heat is so near
Now goodbye and I'll see you
Next summer and that's no lie.

Rebecca O'Hare (11)
St Mary's Immaculate Catholic Primary School, Warwick

Summer

In summer's golden rays,
All the women begin to bathe,
Boisterous boys and giggling girls,
Eat so many sweets, it makes them hurl.

The frightening wasps and bumblebees,
Make us pray for mercy on our knees,
So we all jet off to golden sand,
That is in a distant land.

Dad cooks us all burnt hot dogs,
Then he takes us camping and tries to burn wet logs,
Our ice cream melts too fast
And in six weeks it all becomes the past.

Joshua Sheward (10)
St Mary's Immaculate Catholic Primary School, Warwick

Summer Days

You're climbing a tree
You keep getting higher
You look at yourself
And you're as red as a fire

You look at the sun
It burns so bright
You're glad it isn't
As dark as the night

You go to the beach
In the burning heat
You look at the ground
And see lots of feet

You go in the ocean
And have some fun
You come back out
And you're as wet as a sticky ice bun.

Bradley Holland (10)
St Mary's Immaculate Catholic Primary School, Warwick

Alien

Once I saw an alien
He was green and ugly
He had bigger eyes than mine

I once saw an alien
Sitting on my bed
He said his name was Fred
So I hit him on the head

I once saw a UFO hovering in the sky
It beamed down to Earth
And gave me a fright.

Kerry Rockcliffe (11)
St Mary's Immaculate Catholic Primary School, Warwick

Aliens

The night is calm and serene
But you look up and see something green
Strange faces, different places
Looking down at the ground
Alien life-forces that confirm we are up in space
What a wonderful place
All the people up in space are aliens
Some of them live on Mars
Most of them live in the stars
All the aliens come out to play
But when the night reaches, the aliens hide away
The aliens pop out one last time
To say goodbye to the people on Earth.

Kelsey Atkins (10)
St Mary's Immaculate Catholic Primary School, Warwick

Here On My Plate

Here on my red plate,
I see a house with children in
And a woman dressing her daughter,
A boy playing football with his dog,
The trees are rocking side to side,
As the children play on old wood,
The smoke from the chimney,
Swiftly turning into blackbirds,
Winter's coming, wrap up warm,
The trees moving their branches,
Like arms on a puppet.

Jordan Martin (10)
St Mary's Immaculate Catholic Primary School, Warwick

A Bright, Bright Summer

Come on sun show yourself
Summer is quite near
Let's get our shorts and T-shirts on
And have a pint of beer

Let's put our suncream on at once
So we don't go bright red
For if we get burnt a lot
We'll have to stay in bed

We're going to the beach today
To surf in the sea
But the only thing I'm afraid of is
A shark might bite me.

Matthew Chamberlain (9)
St Mary's Immaculate Catholic Primary School, Warwick

Summer

When the sun is shining
It's always good for rhyming
Children buying water guns
Adults eating hot cross buns
Babies playing in the sand
What a laugh, hold my hand
This is like so much fun
Enjoying the sand and red, red sun
Picnics and sandwiches are all so yummy
Come on Mum, give me some money
The day has gone and I'm going home
It was lots of fun not being alone.

Jade Tunnicliff (10)
St Mary's Immaculate Catholic Primary School, Warwick

SATs

I have to sit my SATs this week,
I feel so sick, I can't even eat,
My helper Tracey is so sweet,
She says don't worry, just find a seat,
I wish an alien would come down from space
And get me out this awful place,
I could have new friends to meet,
I have to sit my SATs this week.

Jodi Griffin (11)
St Mary's Immaculate Catholic Primary School, Warwick

SATs

One term at every school
You have SATs and believe me, it's not cool
You sit on a chair
Thinking it's not fair
With a paper in front of you
Boohoo.

Sarah Allen (11)
St Mary's Immaculate Catholic Primary School, Warwick

Tracy

T racy can be very kind
R arely has a bad mind
A lso she can have a joke
C aring as well
Y ou're mostly right, Tracy.

Harry Young (11)
St Mary's Immaculate Catholic Primary School, Warwick

Summer

The sun is bright as gold,
People on the beaches,
As brown as burnt leaves,
People on the beaches,
Chatting like chatterboxes,
Children playing in pools,
Splashing like water,
Children licking ice cream,
Like dogs with a bone.

Brandon Wareing (10)
St Mary's Immaculate Catholic Primary School, Warwick

The Alien

Spaceship coming from outer space
A big tall alien with an ugly face
He has come to Earth to look at us
His spaceship is like a big red bus
His eyes are black and really big
His body shaped like a twig
I hope he goes back really soon
Towards his planet beyond the moon.

Liam Brooks (11)
St Mary's Immaculate Catholic Primary School, Warwick

Poem About An Alien

Seven-eyed alien big and fat
No place to go but on my back
Running around on my mat
Get him off, let's have a chat.

Stephanie Manning (11)
St Mary's Immaculate Catholic Primary School, Warwick

Tracey!

Tracey is beautiful,
Tracey is kind,
She's always helping,
With her wonderful mind.

She's always smiling,
Everywhere,
She eats her lunch,
Even her pear.

Her favourite idol
Is Robbie Williams,
To see him
She would pay millions.

Katie Emeney (11)
St Mary's Immaculate Catholic Primary School, Warwick

SATs

I sat in awe
And watched the door
I wondered what would come
Comprehension, mathematics
I would rather do gymnastics!
Hope, today, I am not dumb

Papers rustle, pencils sharp,
Clock ticks by, my heart is dark,
Turn the page, it's literacy!
What a lucky day for me!

Jamie Dunbar (10)
St Mary's Immaculate Catholic Primary School, Warwick

Fairies' Ball

Fluttering, flying
Dancing by,
Watch the fairies as they fly.

Fluttering fairies,
Flitter by,
Wings that glisten like drops of ice.

Gowns that sparkle
In the light,
Bright and beautiful as a starry night.

The fairy queen's hair is golden brown,
If you look carefully you can see her crown.

When the moonlight starts to dim,
Dancing again is their only whim,
Retreating to their toadstool homes,
The queen will sit back on her throne.

Ashton Branston (10)
St Oswald's CE Primary School, Rugby

Ten Things Found In A Wizard's Pocket

A rainy night
A picture that nobody could ever colour
A threatening dragon
A chair made from slimy honey
A leaf the size of a mountain
A licence from the post office
A bucketful of sun and wind to mix with a rainy night
Some Cadbury mice with no tails
A frightening owl.

Sujahn Barhey (8)
St Oswald's CE Primary School, Rugby

My Family

I have a mum called Kathy
And she is an A&E nurse,
She makes the best cottage pie
In the entire universe.

I have a dad called Marty
And he is a train driver,
He doesn't carry passengers,
His train is called Freightliner.

I have a sister called Connie
And she goes to school,
She likes to play with dollies
And she is very, very cool.

I have a white Westie called Bob,
He's a very slow mover,
Although he is very small,
We call him the little white hoover.

Now every family has a crazy one
And this one is called Bethany,
Although they drive her up the wall,
She thinks they are really lovely.

Bethany McLaren (10)
St Oswald's CE Primary School, Rugby

A Poem About My Mum

My mum is funny and gives me pocket money,
My mum is fun and plays in the sun,
My mum is cuddly and is warm and snugly,
My mum is lovely and always hugs me,
My mum is friendly and is very trendy,
My mum is great and bakes lovely cakes,
My mum is cool and takes me to school,
My mum is happy and is very chatty!

Jordana Lawes (10)
St Oswald's CE Primary School, Rugby

Too Hot To Play

The sun is shining,
It's too hot to play,
She sat in the house,
On the hot summer's day.

She sat there alone,
She sat there she did
And she said, 'It's too hot to play,
On this hot summer's day.'

Too dry to play out,
Plus too hot to play ball,
So she sat in the house
And did nothing at all.

So all she could do was to . . .
Stare!
    Sit!
        Stare!
She did not like it,
Not one little bit.

Marianne Willey (10)
St Oswald's CE Primary School, Rugby

Ten Things Found In A Wizard's Pocket

A light night
Some letters that God could not spell
A potion that heals people
A large bird
Some beds made out of silk
A pen as big as a road
A bucketful of twisters
A bag of chewing gum you cannot swallow
A bad dog.

Rory Absalom (8)
St Oswald's CE Primary School, Rugby

An Alphabet Of Creepy Creatures

An angry alien attacking
A brutal beagle breaking
A curious calf cracking
A deadly dinosaur dying
An evil elephant eating
A fragile fox feasting
A great giant groaning
A huge hare hearing
An invisible insect investigating
A jumpy jaguar jawing
A crazy koala kung-fuing
A lazy lion lying
A mad mole mealing
A nasty newt neighing
An orange ogre oofing
A picky penguin performing
A quiet quail quacking
A red rabbit roaring
A slow snail slooping
A turquoise tarantula tearing
A useful UFO using
A vain vampire vanishing
A warm whale wailing
An x-rayed xenophobic x-raying
A yellow yak yelling
A zigzagging zebra zooming
These are the creepy creatures.

Alexander Jordan (7)
St Oswald's CE Primary School, Rugby

An Alphabet Of Creepy-Crawlies

An angry alien attacking
A bare bee buzzing
A cute cat crying
A deep dog digging
An enormous eel eating
A floppy fairy fishing
A groovy grandad gurgling
A hot hamster hurting
An itchy insect ironing
A juggling jackdaw jumping
A kidnapper kid kissing
A lovely ladybird lapping
A mad monkey making mud pies
A naked nan knocking
An orange orang-utan omitting
A pale painter painting
A quiet koala quacking
A racing rat rusting
A smiling snake singing
A tired T-rex tap dancing
An ugly unicorn
A violent vampire vaporising
A warfare writer winding
An extreme empire exploding
A young yak yawning
A zealous zebra crossing.

Alice Allett (7)
St Oswald's CE Primary School, Rugby

The Time

Once up on a rhyme,
I had to ask the time.

He said 5 o'clock
And he smelt a stinky sock.

We were there forever,
We were standing alone together.

Soon it turns 7,
And then it was 11.

I said bye-bye,
But he started to cry.

Finally I went to bed
And I had a thumping head.

Zachary Rees (9)
St Oswald's CE Primary School, Rugby

Summer

The boiling sun comes out slowly on hot summer days,
We go by shiny car to large swimming centres,
Get out cool pools speedily and happily play
With huge footballs sportily,
Then we go by speedy car to the sandy seaside,
In comes the wet tide quickly,
We finish hungrily with giant, tasty ice creams,
Go to our warm homes to cuddle up in bed and sleep . . .
Sweet dreams.

Kieran Taylour (10)
St Oswald's CE Primary School, Rugby

On A Day

On a windy day
When the wind was blowing
I wanted to play
So Mum took me bowling

On a sunny day
When the sun was shining
I wanted to play
But the sun was scorching

On a day, a cloudy day
When the rain was falling
I wanted to play
But I was scared of drowning

On a snowy day
When the weather was freezing
We went skiing

On a warm day
We went to play skittles in the garden
And I won.

Rory Hanby (9)
St Oswald's CE Primary School, Rugby

Ten Things Found In A Wizard's Pocket

A cloudy night
Some pencils that cannot break
A jug full of wine
A large hippopotamus
A top made out of net
A pen that is the size of an elephant
A bill from the moon shop
A box of stars and the moon and planets
A flat elephant
A fish that can close his eyes.

Lauren Scott (7)
St Oswald's CE Primary School, Rugby

An Alphabet Of Creepy-Crawlies

An angry alligator attacking
A beautiful beaver burying
A cool crocodile cooling
A deadly dinosaur digging
An enormous eel exaggerating
A fierce fox fearing
A giant giant giggling
An ignorant insect imagining
A juggling jacket juggling
A king kong cunning
A lovely lobster lurking
A mother mongrel muttering
An annoyed newt nodding
An orange orang-utan owning
A pimpled puppy puffing
A quiet quail quacking
A rattling rattlesnake racing
A serious snake smelling
A terrific tarantula trotting
An ugly umpire vibrating
A witty whale weeping
An extreme exterminator examining
A yellow yeti yawning
A zany zombie zooming.

Kyle Cooper (8)
St Oswald's CE Primary School, Rugby

A Recipe For An Elephant Sandwich

An elephant sandwich is easy to make
All you do is simply take
One piece of bread
One piece of chocolate
Some mayonnaise
One cherry
One elephant
One piece of paper
A dash of salt
That ought to do it
And now comes the problem . . .
Biting into it!

Kya Harris (8)
St Oswald's CE Primary School, Rugby

Ten Things Found In A Wizard's Pocket

A cloudy night
Some pencils that could never break
A jug full of wine
A fat pig
A bed made of cobwebs
A cat the size of an ant
A handbag full of sweets from the wand shop
A bucketful of stars and the moon
A bag of poisoned sweets that can turn you into a pig
A black and white owl tooting.

Lauren Ross (8)
St Oswald's CE Primary School, Rugby

Ten Things Found In A Wizard's Pocket

A scary night
Some spells that nobody could cast
A glassful of Malibu
The biggest giraffe in the world
A bed made out of monkey fur
A stone the size of a hotel
A piece of paper with a hundred numbers
A bucketful of monsters to go with the scary night
A bagful of magic Tic-Tacs that will last till the future
A legless owl.

Toni Rotheram (8)
St Oswald's CE Primary School, Rugby

Ten Things Found In A Wizard's Pocket

A gloomy night
A glass of water that nobody could drink out of
A pencil that nobody could snap
A threatening dragon
A terrifying dead mouse
A world that nobody ever knew spun
A book that nobody ever opened
A bottle that nobody drank
A chair that nobody ever broke.

Thomas Branston (8)
St Oswald's CE Primary School, Rugby

Once Upon A Time

Once upon a time
I found a mime,
He gave me a lime,
But I fell in a puddle of slime,
Lucky for me I found a dime,
I've had enough of this rhyme,
I'll try another one next time,
Uh-oh, I've just committed a crime,
Oops that didn't make sense that last line,
I just read a sign,
It said that I was just divine.

Kyle Bowden (10)
St Oswald's CE Primary School, Rugby

Day And Night

The day is so young
The sun shines bright
I love the day
I love the light
The moon comes out
The stars shine bright
I love the dark
I love the night.

Luis Holloway (9)
St Oswald's CE Primary School, Rugby

Ten Things Found In A Wizard's Pocket

A scary thundery night
A curse that nobody could ever get off
A jug of nasty worms
An enormous hippopotamus
A cardigan made from slimy honey
A chair the size of a house
A cheque signed with a feather quill
A bowl with a moon and a half moon
A plastic bag sugary sweet that you can suck forever
A fat elephant.

Shivani Koria (7)
St Oswald's CE Primary School, Rugby

Ten Things Found In A Wizard's Pocket

A dark gloomy night
Some words that nobody could ever spell
A jug that people could never spill
A large hippopotamus
A vest made of silkworms' silk
A 2p the size of a planet
A cheque from the wand shop
A bucketful of zombies and ghosts
A bag of chewing gum that never loses its taste
A freaky owl.

Ciaran Wardle (8)
St Oswald's CE Primary School, Rugby

Ten Things Found In A Wizard's Pocket

A fierce night
Some spells that nobody could ever cast
A scary dragon
A bed made from bird wings
An earring the size of a pharaoh's crown
A signature signed by a wizard with a quill
A bucket of fire, clouds and rain
A packet of bubblegum that nobody could ever chew
A fiery owl.

Ben Romasz (8)
St Oswald's CE Primary School, Rugby

Ten Things Found In A Wizard's Pocket

A sunny night
A photograph that nobody could ever take
A bed full of crawling centipedes
A star big as the world
A clownfish funny as a monkey
A killer whale big as the sea
A wand thin as a toothbrush
A proud looking giraffe
A fat man, fat as a hamburger
A ruler that nobody could measure.

Sarita Sihra (8)
St Oswald's CE Primary School, Rugby

Eloise

There was a young girl called Eloise
Who really liked eating peas
She ate one too many
Turned into a penny!
Only to be spent on some cheese.

Henry Lougher (9)
The Croft School, Stratford-Upon-Avon

The Moon's Dance

The moon flows
Like a silky marshmallow floating in bubbling hot chocolate
Shimmers
Like a fire in a miner's cave
Gallops
Like a shadow in a moonlight's gaze
Sleeps
Like a baby in a blanket where it lay
Drapes
Like a curtain over an icy window
Watches
Like a cat on a brick wall watching his prey.

Ellie Sergeant (11)
The Croft School, Stratford-Upon-Avon

Happiness

Happiness is bright orange
Like the sun on a summer's evening
It tastes like ripe nectarines and peaches
Happiness is the smell of fresh straw
And vanilla milkshakes and it sounds
Like children laughing in a playground
Happiness is super.

Louise Keegan (10)
The Croft School, Stratford-Upon-Avon

A Limerick

There once was a young boy called Jim,
Who wanted to learn how to swim,
He jumped in the pool,
(For he was a fool)
And they had to resuscitate him.

Naomi Nixon (11)
The Croft School, Stratford-Upon-Avon

Snow Is Falling

Snow is falling everywhere,
What a funny sight,
It's not very often,
We see the world so white.

Put your hats and scarves on,
So we can go and play,
Keep yourself snug and warm,
On this winter's day.

Birds are digging low,
So they can find food,
We're drinking hot chocolate,
It is really good.

Elizabeth Cawthorn (10)
The Croft School, Stratford-Upon-Avon

A Street At Night

A street at night is dark,
If you're lucky you could hear a lark,
Or bat's wings fluttering gently
And the revving of a black Bentley.
Your father snoring loudly,
An owl with its prey, hooting proudly,
The barking of an upset dog
And the miaowing of a stray mog,
Or a teenager shouting and staring
At the football on telly, it's blaring.
So switch on your bedside light
And hear the sounds of a street at night!

Lucy Martin (11)
The Croft School, Stratford-Upon-Avon

The Blizzard

The Blizzard
A blender filled with snow.
White, raging, windy
Like a sheet of snow being tossed around.
Like a big breath on a tiny ant
It makes me feel so weak.
Like the strength of an elephant compared to me.
The Blizzard
Reminds me that I am insignificant.

Ian Howard (11)
The Croft School, Stratford-Upon-Avon

Mobile Phone

I am ten years old and want a phone
A mobile, wap, hi-tech 3G,
To text my mates and surf the net
I'll look so cool, I'll look the best
I wish my dad could see the point
He says it's stupid, but he's just old
I'll get my phone and have my fun
Just avoid my dad and ask my mum!

James Page (10)
The Croft School, Stratford-Upon-Avon

Happiness

Happiness smells like vanilla,
Happiness looks like a bright flower,
Happiness tastes of exotic fruits,
Happiness is a big part of me,
And that is how it will always be!

Portia Conn
The Croft School, Stratford-Upon-Avon

My Dog, Sherry

Sherry
s *he* is cute
full of *e* nergy
always *r* eady to play
and *r* un around
y ou are crazy if you do not love her

S herry
s *h* e is a sheepdog
always th *e* re when you want a hug
very *l* oveable with
very *t* hick fur
she is *i* ntelligent and
perfect in *e* very way and form.

Andrew Turton (10)
The Croft School, Stratford-Upon-Avon

The Cat

Eyes aglow, staring into the night,
A luminous yellow, the cat's eyes are bright,
Soft and warm and smooth is his fur,
When I stroke him he miaows a soft purr.

He sits very still watching prey scuttle past,
He bares his claws ready, then pounces fast,
The cat's very angry because he has missed
And does the equivalent to clenching his fist.

Eyes aglow, staring into the night,
A luminous yellow, the cat's eyes are bright.

Felicity Box (11)
The Croft School, Stratford-Upon-Avon

The Spring Tulip

Each spring day I'm glad to say
The tulip's up and ready to play
Then in the night the tulip's petals flop
As though going to drop right off
But no, no, that can't be right
Even though it's quiet at night
Then sun!
The tulip opens up when day's begun
Glistening, swaying, attracting the bees
Like a sugarplum fairy with shimmering leaves
Its colourful glint it gives away
Never leaves any spring day
Then winter comes, the tulip wilts
Then tilts, tilts, tilts
The cool wind blows and all goes dry
The orange leaves whirl around the sky
Then after the rain
The spring comes twinkling back again
Then in the golden sunlit ray
The tulip pops right up to play.

Jenny Morris (11)
The Croft School, Stratford-Upon-Avon

Football

Football, football
Game of the season
Everyone played throughout
The summer for no reason
Oh how I'd love
To play football every day
But by the time I get to the pitch
It's the end of play!

Jamie Thomas (10)
The Croft School, Stratford-Upon-Avon

Limericks

There once was a rap star named Mark
Who was very afraid of the dark
The lights went out
So he started to shout
Now he sings like a lark

There once was a boy named Charlie
Who celebrated the day of Diwali
He ate fish and chips
Instead of Indian bots and bits
He now drinks lemon barley

There once was a boy named Ed
Who had a very large head
He had large feet
As he ate lots of meat
So now he has a huge bed.

Mark Tagliaferri (11)
The Croft School, Stratford-Upon-Avon

Twister

A twister . . .
Spins
    like cold water going down a plughole
Amazes
    like a magic land of doom and death
Destroys
    like a giant disease spreading and killing
Devastates
    like a relation in pain about to die
And kills
    like an amputation in progress.

Ellie Forman (10)
The Croft School, Stratford-Upon-Avon

Sport

I'll shoot that football,
I will smack that cricket ball,
I'll run that distance.

One day I'll be great,
I will be the very best,
I'll beat everyone.

As the Titans clash,
I will be in the middle,
Holding up the cup.

When aliens come
To represent their planets,
Of course I'll be there.

Aliens will cheat
And for sure I won't need to,
I'll win for our Earth.

Peter Walters (11)
The Croft School, Stratford-Upon-Avon

Sport

Playing football on a sunny day
Is a fantastic way to play,
Kick a football so, so high
And watch it glide in the sky,
When it comes down you will get
To see the ball in the back of the net,
I also like cricket too
And I like to play just me and you,
Bowl a ball so very fast
And get them out to the last,
Hit a ball along the ground
And make sure to give it some pound,
Have a good day of sport
And try not to get nought.

Alex Hughes (10)
The Croft School, Stratford-Upon-Avon

Dance

Can you ballet dance,
So slender and smooth?
Can you rock dance,
Getting in the groove?

Can you tap dance,
Click, click, click?
Can you line dance,
Stamp, clap, kick?

Can you do the salsa,
So quick and alive?
Can you water dance,
Jump, leap, dive?

Can you do the cha-cha-cha,
Clap, kick, kick?
Can you do the tango?
You must be quick!

Can you waltz,
Stylish and slow?
Can you do aerobics,
See how long you can go?

Can you dance?

Catherine Lawler (11)
The Croft School, Stratford-Upon-Avon

Happiness

Happiness is a yellow sunflower,
It tastes of melted chocolate,
Happiness smells of perfumed lavender
And looks like a round smiling sun,
It sounds like the chirping of little birds,
Happiness feels like the soft sand sliding through your toes,
Happiness is delightful!

Emma Walshe (10)
The Croft School, Stratford-Upon-Avon

Tobogganing

Down that slope so steep and white,
Staying out till late at night,
Zooming down with all my friends,
The fun never seems to end,
Whoosh, skid, slip, slide,
Down that hill we all ride,
We drag our toboggans back up the hill
And down we go to get our fill.

Mark Dove (11)
The Croft School, Stratford-Upon-Avon

Granddaughter's Fear

When Granddaughter is petrified, fearful and scared,
She clings to her grandmother tight,
So Grandmother sings an encouraging song,
A song that lasts all of the night!

Soaring hawks scare Granddaughter,
As well as the toucans and cats,
She is scared of foxes, armadillos,
Especially the little black bats!

Granddaughter is hardly ever vicious,
Her heart is loaded with her fear,
She runs to her caring grandmother,
Who says, 'Don't be scared my dear.'

They live halfway up the mountain,
Near there is a river so smooth,
When Granddaughter is with her grandmother,
Her fears begin to soothe!

Emily Aveyard
Welford On Avon Primary School, Stratford-Upon-Avon

Grandmother's Song

Hawks soaring
Toucans cawing
Discover your fear
And spirits very near

Dance in the sun
The day has begun
It is very hot
And they cook with a pot

Grandmother
Who hates to bother
Granddaughter
Who hates manslaughter

Mexico has hot weather
Nothing made of leather
People are daring
But some are caring.

Daniel Walsh (9)
Welford On Avon Primary School, Stratford-Upon-Avon

Grandmother

Grandmother lives in Mexico,
Where toucans and hawks swoop so low,
So much hot weather,
In Mexico life goes on forever.

Caring for her scared granddaughter,
Shivering about by the water,
Singing a beautiful song,
To overcome fears for so long.

Grandmother's spirit is all around,
Singing a song with a lovely sound,
Living in the countryside,
Where granddaughter's mother died.

Eleanor Johnston (10)
Welford On Avon Primary School, Stratford-Upon-Avon

Grandmother's Song

Grandmother is very powerful,
Grandmother is very hopeful,
She is kind,
Spirit all around.

Mexico is hot,
Very hot,
Her granddaughter's scared
And afraid.

Grandmother sings a song,
Each time her granddaughter's gone,
To see the scary things.

Mexico is hot,
Very hot,
Her granddaughter's scared
And afraid.

Jessica Summer (9)
Welford On Avon Primary School, Stratford-Upon-Avon

Grandmother Helps Granddaughter

Grandmother's granddaughter is scared
With fear in her eyes
They're dripping down with a tear
It's Mexico so it is very hot
I don't think it would rain a lot

Grandmother is powerful, caring and kind
It's just like Granddaughter is slipping behind
Soon Grandmother told Granddaughter how to believe in herself
And then Granddaughter doesn't walk around
With her eyes closed and knock stuff off the shelf
Grandmother told Granddaughter how to be brave
They tested it out in a cave.

Harry White (9)
Welford On Avon Primary School, Stratford-Upon-Avon

Grandmother And Granddaughter

Grandmother's spirit in Mexico
Is all around us from head to toe,
For Granddaughter is normally scared,
But not when she knows she's being cared.

The fear of Granddaughter,
The kindness of Grandma,
The sound of the hawk and bird,
We know very little by far.

But even we must move on now,
Because it's time for you to see,
That time moves on
And Grandmother will be gone,
In years of stroking, singing and calming.

But Granddaughter is now Grandmother
And a strong one she is,
When she sings and sings
And strokes and strokes,
Her grandchildren think they are kings.

Lucas Spence
Welford On Avon Primary School, Stratford-Upon-Avon

Grandmother's Song

Grandmother is caring and loving and kind
She would never leave Granddaughter behind
Granddaughter is a scaredy-cat
She's even scared of other children
Fancy that!
But Grandmother is always there to help her
She cares, is powerful and loves her
But soon grandmother will die
And Granddaughter will be sad
But Grandmother's spirit will live on
And for that Granddaughter is glad.

Jennifer Lane (9)
Welford On Avon Primary School, Stratford-Upon-Avon

Grandmother

There's spirits all around and fear
So why don't you overcome it?
Granddaughter is very scared
But Grandmother is very caring
I'm making lots of lovely corn

Grandmother is rubbing all of the fear
Out of Granddaughter's heart
So Granddaughter has a part
So goodbye to all of the fear
From Granddaughter

Granddaughter rubs trust into me
So Granddaughter has trust for life
Granddaughter is very scared
But Grandmother is rubbing confidence into her.

Morgan Jackson (9)
Welford On Avon Primary School, Stratford-Upon-Avon

Grandmother's Song

Grandmother is caring
But she is a bit wearing
There are a lot of hawks
And a lot of walks

They think that life is forever
Whatever the weather
It may be hot
But hawks are not

The mountains are big
They have to dig
They eat lots of food
Even in a bad mood.

James Clifford (9)
Welford On Avon Primary School, Stratford-Upon-Avon